LORD'S CRICKET GROUND IN 50 MEMORIALS

STEVEN MIELL

AMBERLEY

Cover photographs by Jed Leicester

First published 2026

Amberley Publishing
The Hill, Stroud
Gloucestershire, GL5 4EP

www.amberley-books.com

ISBN 978 1 3981 2792 0 (print)
ISBN 978 1 3981 2793 7 (ebook)

British Library Cataloguing in Publication Data.
A catalogue record for this book is available from the British Library.

Typesetting by SJmagic DESIGN SERVICES, India.
Printed in Great Britain.

Appointed GPSR EU Representative: Easy Access System Europe Oü, 16879218
Address: Mustamäe tee 50, 10621, Tallinn, Estonia
Contact Details: gpsr.requests@easproject.com, +358 40 500 3575

CONTENTS

FOREWORDS

The job of a Tour Guide is a multi-faceted one: actor, public-speaker, storyteller, security guard, public relations officer. All these skills are needed, but there is one further quality that marks out the best guides, and the best historians. That quality is curiosity. Curiosity is the difference between someone who merely repeats an established story – although they might do it in a very entertaining way – and someone who is willing to dig deeper to establish the truth and get to the heart of a story.

This book is a tribute to the author's curiosity. I have had the pleasure of helping Steven at various stages of preparing this work, and I know how meticulous he has been in digging out the facts. Steven has not simply parroted the well-worn narratives that have been published in various histories of Lord's over the years, he has checked and double-checked, researching every conceivable aspect of the stories he tells to make certain they are as authentic as possible.

On the way, he has uncovered some gems of information that even surprised me, after almost two decades working at Lord's. This book may not bear the stamp of an officially authorised history of Lord's Cricket Ground, but that doesn't make it any less authoritative. I am sure the reader will find plenty to surprise and enjoy in the pages that follow.

Neil Robinson
Head of Heritage and Collections at Marylebone Cricket Club

Since joining Middlesex CCC in 1972, I have played many times at this famous old cricket ground. From county games with sparse attendances to major one-day finals with sell-out crowds, I have become well-acquainted with the venue.

After retiring as a first-class cricketer, I have had numerous opportunities to return to Lord's. Most recently, I have been fortunate to be able to share my experiences of playing at Lord's with groups of visitors on tours led by the author (and my long-time friend) Steve Miell. Despite my extensive experience playing at Lord's, I have gained a great deal of knowledge about the Ground and its history by listening to Steve. I am pleased to see that he has compiled his knowledge and insights into a book, which highlights fifty areas – some well-known and others less so.

Steve's book is a great way to get to know Lord's Cricket Ground and to understand its role in cricket history.

Roland Butcher
Middlesex CCC and England

INTRODUCTION

Lord's Cricket Ground, the home of Marylebone Cricket Club (MCC), is situated in St John's Wood, a leafy suburb in North West London. For over 200 years, the current Lord's Ground has been a place of significant memories and mystique. The word 'iconic' has been defined as 'widely known and acknowledged especially for distinctive excellence'. This definition certainly applies to Lord's Cricket Ground, a venue synonymous with cricket history and traditions.

I became an MCC Member in 1985 and, since 2019, I have had the privilege of working at Lord's as a Tour Guide. However, my association with the Ground goes back much further. My first visit there was on 1 September 1973, when I watched Gloucestershire beat Sussex to win the Gillette Cup, the world's first one-day domestic cricket knockout competition. I clearly remember the pace and aggression of John Snow, the swagger of Tony Greig, and the all-round ability of Mike Procter. At that time, my involvement with Gloucestershire allowed me to enjoy the subsequent celebrations at the Gloucestershire Chairman's residence.

Since that first visit in 1973, the Ground has undergone significant changes. Around the boundary, only the magnificent Victorian Pavilion, the Bowlers' Bar, the Tavern Stand, and the Allen Stand (or, for older members, 'Q' Stand) remain from that time. However, the numerous changes to the locations from which a spectator can watch cricket have only enhanced the Ground's unique aura.

Lord's boasts a distinctive atmosphere and a rich history that is unique among sports grounds around the world. On and within its walls, numerous stories about the people, their exploits, and the structures that have contributed to the Ground's development can be recounted. These include the celebrated Test match Honours Boards, situated in the players' dressing rooms, along with more recent additions such as the Heyhoe Flint Gate, and a plaque to commemorate the spot where the Women's Ashes was created.

This book invites the reader to learn more about fifty of the better-known, as well as some lesser-known, memorials, commemorations and other objects found at Lord's Ground. These include statues and busts, war memorials, stands, and other buildings, and the people who have inspired them. I have avoided the more obvious items, such as the original Ashes Urn and the cricket balls with which the Australian bowler Bob Massie took sixteen wickets in one Ashes Test match. This process has also led me down a few 'rabbit holes'. For example, when writing about the Grace Gates – constructed to commemorate the life of W. G. Grace – I wanted to write briefly about Sir Stanley Jackson, a playing contemporary of W. G.'s, who unveiled the Gates in 1922. Additionally, in discussing the Pavilion, I have included more detail about the architect, Thomas Verity.

The book begins with the first two Lord's Grounds – the 'New' and the 'Middle' Grounds – and then continues with the outer walls of the present Ground. Once inside the Ground, there are features in the gardens and on the exterior of the Pavilion. From there, into the Museum, followed by an overview of the stands. Other areas around the Ground are looked at before returning to the Pavilion's interior, describing various items contained within, and the stories behind them.

Each of the fifty areas chosen, whether large like the Media Centre, or small like the unfortunate Lord's Sparrow, has its own story, sometimes overlooked when the history of the Ground is written. It is hoped that the reader's interest will be piqued to learn more about both MCC's and the Ground's history.

MCC'S ORIGINS

How did Marylebone Cricket Club – a private Members' Club and the owners of Lord's Ground – end up in St John's Wood? Two individuals were pivotal in the early development of cricket in general, and of MCC in particular. The first – George Finch – was born on 4 November 1752 in the Westminster area of London.

George Finch

Finch was educated at Eton College, and in 1769, at the age of seventeen, he inherited the title of 9th Earl of Winchilsea from his childless uncle, Daniel Finch, the 8th Earl of Winchilsea and 3rd Earl of Nottingham. The title came with the 8th Earl's estate at Burley-on-the-Hill, Rutland.

Winchilsea graduated from Christ Church College in Oxford in 1771. When the American War of Independence broke out in April 1775, he helped to form the 87th Foot Regiment. He saw active service with the unit until it was disbanded when hostilities ended in September 1783. He had attained the temporary rank of major and, later, lieutenant-colonel. When he returned from America, Winchilsea was in his early thirties.

Nathaniel Dance-Holland's 1771 portrait of George Finch (9th Earl of Winchilsea) at Oxford University. (MCC)

By 1784, Winchilsea had become a driving force behind the White Conduit Club. Formed in the early 1780s in the Islington area to the north of London, the White Conduit Club was a cricket club and an offshoot of the convivial 'Je-ne-sais-quoi' Club – also known as the Star & Garter Club, named after the tavern in Pall Mall, where its members used to gather. The White Conduit Club* employed professional cricketers to coach the players, maintain the ground and bowl to the more privileged members.

*White Conduit Club

In the sixteenth century, around 500 people lived in the Islington area. The fields in the vicinity were notorious for criminal behaviour and for other activities, including militia training, organised duels, and sporting events.

It is believed that the White Conduit Club was located near the King's Cross area of north London, close to White Conduit House, which was in (now) Penton Street. The house was named after a water conduit that had supplied Carthusian friars since the late fifteenth century. In 1754, White Conduit House was advertised as having several attractions, including 'copious prospects, and airy situation'. In addition, visitors could experience 'a long walk, a circular fishpond, a number of pleasant shady arbours, hot loaves and butter, milk direct from the cow, coffee, tea, and other liquors, a cricket field, unadulterated cream, and a handsome long room, enclosed with a fence seven feet high'. The area became popular with Londoners anxious to escape the city.

By the mid-eighteenth century, cricket had emerged as the predominant sport in the area. Younger aristocrats enjoyed playing cricket, drinking alcohol, and gambling. Indeed, gambling played a significant role in cricket's early days, and it was not uncommon for wagers exceeding 1,000 guineas (around £100,000 in today's terms) to be placed on a single match, often accompanied by side bets.

Any evidence of the original location has been lost over the years beneath London's urban development.

On 23 November 1755, just over three years after the birth of George Finch, Thomas Lord, the second of the two influential figures who played a significant role in the formation, development and growth of MCC in its early years, was born in Thirsk, Yorkshire.

Thomas Lord

Thomas Lord was the son of Roman Catholic parents whose land had been sequestered in 1745 because they supported the Jacobite uprisings. Lord's father was a 'yeoman'– a gentleman farmer – who could only find paid work as a labourer on (what was) his property following the seizure of his lands.

Later, the family moved to Diss in Norfolk, where Thomas Lord was brought up. Lord found it difficult to settle in Norfolk and when he reached adulthood, he relocated to London.

Portrait of Thomas Lord by an unknown artist. (MCC)

In the early 1780s, at the age of around twenty-five, Lord had secured a position as an attendant, coach, and practice bowler at the newly formed White Conduit Club in Islington. In contemporary accounts, Lord was described as 'handsome, a capable cricketer, and full of bonhomie'. He was also an entrepreneur and a wine dealer, having supplied wine to the Royal family. Lord became recognised for his business acumen as well as for his cricketing ability and, while he was passionate about cricket, he was also aware of the potential of turning his passion into a business opportunity.

The White Conduit Club's cricketing activities soon encountered problems with the ground in Islington, primarily because it was not enclosed. This allowed the locals to gather en masse and offer 'unsolicited advice' to the players. This situation was even noted in the press at the time. On 22 June 1785, the *Daily Universal Register* reported:

> It is recommended to the Lordling Cricketters who amuse themselves in White Conduit Fields, to procure an Act of Parliament for inclosing their play ground, which will not only prevent their being incommoded, but protect themselves from a repetition of the severe rebuke which they justly merit, and received on Saturday evening from some spirited citizens whom they insulted and attempted vi et armis to drive from the foot path, pretending it was within their bounds.

The club's regular players began to lobby for a move to a more agreeable and convenient location. After all, why should the gentlemen of central and west London travel to this obscure outpost to the north of London, risking the unwanted attention of highwaymen during their journey? The leaders of the White Conduit Club decided to search for a more private venue of their own.

Thomas Lord's attitude, entrepreneurial spirit and ability caught the attention of George Finch, 9th Earl of Winchilsea, and Charles Lennox, 4th Duke of Richmond. As senior members of the White Conduit Club, they identified Lord as the person they could trust with their ambition of finding a new home for their club. They also offered Lord a guarantee against any potential losses he might incur.

Bolstered by this support, in May 1787, Lord leased 7 acres in Dorset Fields, to the west of Baker Street, and situated in the parish of the Church of St Marylebone in London. The landlord was the Portman Estate*, and the site is now the location of Dorset Square.

*The Portman Estate

Founded in 1532, the Portman Estate covers around 110 acres of the Marylebone area in London. The land was initially leased to Sir William Portman, who served as Lord Chief Justice under King Henry VIII. At that time, Portman, originally from the village of Orchard Portman in Somerset, leased 270 acres of the area now known as Lisson.

Around 1550, Portman purchased the freehold of the land, which was predominantly farmland and meadow. It remained as agricultural land until the building boom of the mid-eighteenth century, when Portman Square was developed. The area attracted London's wealthier individuals who wanted to live in pleasant surroundings near the centre of London.

Close to the present-day Marble Arch, and included in the Portman Estate, was Tyburn gallows – London's best-known public execution site until 1783, a few short years before Thomas Lord took the lease on Dorset Fields. It has been estimated that over 50,000 people had been executed there since the 1400s. The last person to be executed at Tyburn was a highwayman, John Austin, on 7 November 1783, for the murder of labourer John Kent. Following Austin's execution, the *Kentish Gazette* reported:

> The mode of taking criminals to Tyburn, and of executing them there, has long been complained of as productive of idleness and vice, instead of inspiring the spectators with awful sentiments, and intimidating them from the commission of heinous crimes and offences. We are happy therefore to inform our readers, that a plan is in the possession of some respectable members of the Corporation of London, for rendering this serious, but necessary ceremony, more striking and efficacious: the outlines of it are as follow :—A temporary scaffold is to be erected opposite the jail of Newgate. The prisoners are to be brought out on the day of execution, and there undergo the sentence of the law.

After 1783, executions were carried out at Newgate prison – now the Old Bailey.

Lord began preparing the new ground at Dorset Fields. He surrounded the site with a fence and, ever the entrepreneur, ensured that his wine store was positioned at the entrance to maximise sales. He also devised the idea of charging an admission fee. By the early summer of 1787, when Thomas Lord was thirty-two years old, the ground was ready for its first cricket match.

The *Morning Herald* of 19 May 1787 included the following announcement:

> A grand match will be played on Monday, 21 May in the New Cricket Ground, the New Road, Mary-le-bone, between eleven Noblemen of the White Conduit Club and eleven Gentlemen of the County of Middlesex with two men given, for 500 guineas a side. The wickets to be pitched at ten o'clock, and the match to be played out.

Thomas Lord's 'New Ground' was up and running, and on 20 June 1787, the first 'Great Match' was played on the Ground in Dorset Fields. This was a three-day game between the White Conduit Club and an All-England team. In keeping with the gambling traditions of the game at the time, wagers were reportedly placed to the tune of 1,000 guineas. For the record, the All-England team won the match by 265 runs. The Earl of Winchilsea captained the White Conduit Club, and the game was notable for the first-class debut of William 'Silver Billy' Beldham, one of the finest and most popular batsmen of his day. A report in *The Daily Universal Register* (later to become *The Times*) on 22 June 1787 claimed that 'upwards of 2,000 persons were within the ground, who conducted themselves with the utmost decorum; the utility of the batten fence was evident, as it kept out all improper spectators'. The ground's surface was described as 'somewhat rough', but there was a promise that it would be laid out the following year 'like a bowling-green'.

The following month, an announcement appeared in *The World* newspaper stating that 'On Monday, 30 July will be played (at Lord's) a match between 11 gentlemen of the Mary-le-bone Club and 11 gentlemen of the Islington Club' (also known as the White Conduit Club). This appears to be the first documented mention of the Marylebone Club in connection with cricket. During the winter of 1787/88, the Members had transformed the old White Conduit Club into a new one named Marylebone Cricket Club. This change formally ended the White Conduit Club and established the supremacy of MCC in English cricket. By 1788, MCC had issued the first codified Laws of Cricket and had emerged as cricket's leading authority, taking over from the Hampshire-based Hambledon Club.

To provide historical context, in the same year that MCC was founded, William Pitt the Younger was the UK's Prime Minister, the Constitution of the United States was signed, and the first fleet of ships sailed to Australia carrying convicts from the United Kingdom who had been sentenced to transportation. George III (1760–1820) was the reigning monarch, and it was a period when the British Empire was rapidly expanding, driven by a spirit of exploration and adventure. Thomas Lord's entrepreneurial attitude seemed to resonate with the spirit of the time. The following year, the Storming of the Bastille signalled the start of the French Revolutionary Wars and the rise of Napoleon Bonaparte.

'NEW' AND 'MIDDLE' GROUNDS

1. Thomas Lord's First (New) Ground

Located in what is now known as Dorset Square in West London, two plaques commemorate the site of Thomas Lord's first Ground. When Lord relocated the White Conduit Club to this location, the area was known as Dorset Fields. This first, or 'New' Ground, is situated approximately 1 mile southeast of the current Lord's Ground.

By the early 1790s, Lord's Ground was well established and recognised as the principal venue in London for cricket matches, often played for substantial sums of money, primarily involving aristocrats and gentlemen. Later in the decade and into the early 1800s, Lord's New Ground hosted several other activities in addition to cricket. For example, in 1799, a military parade was held on Lord's Ground, prompted by fears of an invasion by Napoleon Bonaparte's forces. These fears loomed large, and such parades were common during this period.

On 5 July 1805, French balloonist André-Jacques Garnerin demonstrated a balloon ascent at Lord's Ground. The balloonist ended up in Chingford — then in Essex – covering a distance of around 17 miles in approximately fifteen minutes. Additionally, the Ground was used for pigeon shooting and even hopping competitions.

In 1805, the inaugural match between Eton and Harrow schools was staged at Dorset Fields, with Lord Byron representing Harrow. His performance was far from spectacular, scoring just seven runs and two runs. However, he did take one wicket. The following year, the first Gentlemen versus Players match took place here.

There are two plaques at the site commemorating Thomas Lord's first cricket Ground. The first was placed there to commemorate 1787, the year when Thomas Lord moved the White Conduit Club to the Dorset Fields site. The second plaque – unveiled by MCC's President Colin Cowdrey in June 1987 – marks the passing of 200 years since the first match at Dorset Fields.

With the rapid expansion of London in the early nineteenth century, rising rents made it financially untenable for MCC to remain at Dorset Fields. Thomas Lord began to look for an alternative ground, and on 15 October 1808, he signed an agreement to lease The Brick Field and The Great Field at North Bank in St John's Wood from Henry Samuel Eyre for a period of eighty years. This new site became known as Lord's 'Middle Ground' and was located approximately 300 yards from the present ground. Within a year, the Middle Ground had been prepared for the move.

By 1810, there were two Lord's Grounds. During this brief period, Marylebone Cricket Club continued to play at Lord's New Ground in Dorset Fields, while the St John's Wood Cricket Club played at Lord's Middle Ground. The last game at Lord's New Ground took place on 17 August 1810. An advertisement from that time announced that Lord's second Ground would be called 'Lord's Saint John's Wood Cricket Ground'. The first

Above left: Commemorating Thomas Lord's 'New' Ground in Dorset Fields. (JL)

Above right: Commemorating the bicentenary of the first match played there. (JL)

games there were played by the St John's Wood Cricket Club, which merged into MCC later that year.

2. The Middle Ground

A short walk south along Lisson Grove from the current Ground in St John's Wood is a plaque commemorating the site of Thomas Lord's second cricket Ground – the so-called 'Middle' Ground – following the move from Dorset Fields. Thomas Lord took the turf from Dorset Fields and re-laid it at the Middle Ground, which opened on 8 May 1811.

Following the example set at Lord's first Ground in Dorset Fields, the new site hosted various events, including foot races and pigeon-shooting matches. However, only a handful of cricket matches were ever played there, and MCC's time at the Middle Ground was to be short-lived as, in 1813, Parliament requisitioned the land to enable the construction of the Regent's Canal. The canal would cut through the site, necessitating a further move. Indeed, as early as 28 September 1811, the *Oxford University and City Herald* reported that plans were afoot 'to make a Canal, to be called "The Regent's Canal," from the Grand Junction Canal at Paddington, to communicate with the River Thames, in the parish of Limehouse; and also with the collateral branches'. In a few short years, the *New Times* reported on 16 April 1819 that the new Canal was 'advancing with such rapidity towards a conclusion, that in less than a twelvemonth, it is said, it will be perfectly navigable and complete for all the purposes at trade'. In July 1813, Thomas Lord transferred the ownership of The Middle Ground to Messrs Munro, John Delafield, and John Nash.

In 1814, Lord, who was then fifty-nine years old, once again moved his 'hallowed turf' from the Middle Ground to its present location in St John's Wood. The first Pavilion, a Tavern, and other small buildings were erected on the Ground, and the entire site was

Commemorating the 'Middle Ground' in Lisson Grove. (JL)

enclosed by a high fence. On 2 May 1814, it was announced that all was ready, and the first match took place there on 22 June 1814, when MCC played against Hertfordshire.

This watercolour architectural drawing was created by W. H. Slatter in 1902 for Frank Verity – the son of Thomas Verity, architect of the present Pavilion. It depicts the locations of the three Lord's Grounds. The drawing was donated to MCC by Sir George (Gubby) Allen, a senior figure at Lord's for many years (see Numbers 21 and 31).

The first (or 'New') Ground, located in Dorset Fields, is displayed to the right of the drawing, with the present Dorset Square superimposed on the original Ground's site. The second (or 'Middle') Ground is at the centre of the drawing and clearly illustrates the development that led to the move to the present Ground. The construction of the Regent's Canal and the numerous railway lines in the area resulted in a very brief stay at this location. The present Ground, positioned on the left, is by far the largest of the three. Originally 9 acres in size, the site has been developed and expanded since the move in 1814 and is now approximately 20 acres.

Thomas Lord retired from Lord's Ground in early 1824 when William Ward, a successful financier, renowned cricketer, director of the Bank of England, and Member of Parliament, purchased the remainder of the lease from him for £5,000. During the 1820s, the St John's Wood area experienced significant growth and property development. On 28 July 1825, a fire in Lord's first wooden pavilion created an opportunity to develop part of the Ground for housing. The plans at that time indicated there would have been little room for cricket following any sale. However, the plan did not proceed, and in 1835, William Ward sold the leasehold of the Ground to James Dark, who paid Ward £2,000

The location of all three Lord's Grounds. (JL)

plus an annuity of £425 for the Ward family, which was to last for the unexpired term of the lease – a further fifty-nine years. The freehold of the Ground was eventually bought by MCC in 1866.

After more than forty years of being one of the major forces behind the creation of MCC and the founder of three 'Lord's Grounds', Thomas Lord retired to a farm near the village of West Meon in Hampshire. He died at East End Villa on 18 January 1832 and is buried in West Meon Churchyard.

George Finch, the 9th Earl of Winchilsea and the person who recognised Thomas Lord's flair for business, died on 2 August 1826 at his home in Westminster, London. The *Morning Post* of 5 August 1826 wrote of the:

> Death of the Earl of Winchilsea. — Died at his house in South-street, on Wednesday the 2d inst. in his 74th year, the Right Hon. George Finch, Earl of Winchilsea, K.G. Viscount Maidstone, Baron Finch of Daventry, and Baronet, Lord Lieutenant and Custos Rotulorum of the county of Rutland. His Lordship held the different offices of Lord of the Bedchamber and Groom of the Stole to the late King for nearly thirty years, and was Comptroller of the Windsor Establishment till the decease of his Majesty.

He was buried at Ravenstone, his Buckinghamshire estate.

OUTSIDE THE GROUND

Today's Lord's Ground is situated approximately 300 yards north of the site of the Middle Ground and is bordered on three sides by Grove End Road, St John's Wood Road, and Wellington Road. The southern exterior of Lord's Cricket Ground faces St John's Wood Road, where the main entrance for MCC Members, the Grace Gates, is located. Several items related to the Ground's development can be found along St John's Wood Road, starting at the eastern end of the Ground and extending towards the Grace Gates.

3. Stone Sport Frieze

At the easternmost point of the Ground is a Sport Frieze. The bas-relief frieze was sculpted by Gilbert Bayes, is constructed of Portland stone, and was unveiled in 1934. The *Hampstead News* of 19 July 1934 described the event:

> The Mayor of St. Marylebone (Alderman J. Fettes) unveiled, on Tuesday morning, a notable mural picture outside Lord's Cricket Ground. The sculpture has been erected at the junction of Wellington Road and St. John's Wood Road, is in low relief, and represents 'Sport' and bears the inscription 'Play up, and Play the Game'. We hear that Mr. D. Isaacs, a member of the St. Marylebone Borough Council, is defraying the cost. The work has been executed by Mr. Gilbert Bayes, in his studio, 4 Greville Road, St. John's Wood. The opportunity to erect the frieze was taken when the road frontage at the spot was altered through a road Widening Scheme by Alderman David Isaacs near to its current location.

This art deco relief sculpture depicts a series of sportsmen and women, all shown in contemporary clothing and displaying various pieces of equipment associated with their respective sports. From left to right, the thirteen figures represent tennis, golf, cricket, rugby, football, rowing, and swimming. One of the cricketers is portrayed holding the 'Ashes Urn' and showing it to a second cricketer. The Urn itself had only been presented to MCC by Lord Darnley's widow a few years earlier, in 1928. In the centre of the piece, a man is drying himself with a towel. A third cricketer is depicted on his knees, apparently repairing his bat.

There are several inscriptions on the frieze, as follows:

LORD'S CRICKET GROUND (above the figures' heads)

PLAY UP PLAY UP AND PLAY THE GAME (behind the heads)

Presented to St Marylebone by Alderman David Isaacs 1934 (to the left, below the figures)

Gilbert Bayes, 1934 (just above the swimmer's foot on the extreme right)

The Lord's Sport Frieze. (JL)

In the mid-1990s, due to increased traffic on Wellington and St John's Wood roads, both roads were widened. Consequently, the corner was redesigned, which led to the frieze being placed in its current position.

The quote at the top of the frieze – PLAY UP PLAY UP AND PLAY THE GAME – is from Sir Henry Newbolt's 1897 poem *Vitaï Lampada*. The poem begins with these famous lines:

There's a breathless hush in the Close to-night
Ten to make and the match to win —
A bumping pitch and a blinding light,
An hour to play and the last man in.

The poem celebrates fair play and sportsmanship, urging individuals to remain resolute in times of adversity. It references war, influenced by the patriotism prevalent during the South African War and later during the First World War. The poem explores war as a metaphor for life's challenges and addresses young men in late Victorian Britain who were taught from a young age to adhere to certain sporting values – 'Play the game'. It follows a young man's journey from playing cricket at school (Clifton College in Bristol) to the battlefield.

4. Heyhoe Flint Gate

Continuing along St John's Wood Road in a southerly direction is the fourth item in this series – a set of gates situated between the Stone Sport Frieze and the Bicentenary Gates.

The Heyhoe Flint Gate bas-relief. (JL)

These gates, unveiled on 17 August 2022, honour the life and significant contributions to cricket of Baroness Rachael Heyhoe Flint.

Robert Hunt, a council member, honorary secretary, and trustee of the Society of Portrait Sculptors, designed the bas-relief. Specialising in portraits, he has completed over seventy commissions to date. His notable works include a bust of Professor Jacob Bronowski at Jesus College, Cambridge, and a commemorative relief portrait of the English nurse Edith Cavell for the University of East Anglia, which marked one hundred years since her execution in 1915 during the First World War.

When I asked Robert Hunt about the process leading to his commission for this work, he kindly provided me with the following details from his original proposal:

> The relief portrait will be created within a circle of bronze set into a square of Portland stone. It is felt that a background of pale stone would show off the bronze portrait better than if it were mounted direct onto the weathered brick wall. The plaque will be rectangular in shape, separated from and below the portrait.
>
> So many photographs of Rachael Heyhoe Flint are of a smiling or laughing face, which surely summed up a core part of her character. For a permanent portrait, the recommendation is for a more contemplative face, certainly showing a hint of a smile and at the same time displaying a look of attention and of interest. The one chosen was in a Midland newspaper article, where she is shown with her friend, the comedian Jasper Carrot, who wrote her obituary.

Rachael Heyhoe Flint was a major driving force in the development of cricket in general, and women's cricket in particular, during the second half of the twentieth century. As a player, she made her debut for England in 1960 and served as captain of the England women's team from 1966 to 1978. Under her captaincy, England went unbeaten in six Test series.

Heyhoe Flint, along with businessman and philanthropist Sir Jack Hayward, was responsible for organising the first-ever cricket World Cup – the women's tournament in 1973 – two years before the first men's event in 1975. She captained England to victory in that tournament, with the final played at Edgbaston in Birmingham. On 4 August 1976, during that long hot summer, she led the England team out at Lord's for the first-ever women's match to be staged there. Heyhoe Flint later admitted to feeling emotionally overwhelmed as she stepped onto the outfield.

Heyhoe Flint became one of this country's most respected and best-known sportswomen and was the first woman inducted into the International Cricket Council's (ICC) Hall of Fame in 2010. However, it was in recognition of her extensive work as a charity fundraiser that she was made a Conservative life peer in 2011. Previously, she had been honoured with an MBE in 1972 and an OBE in 2008.

In the 1990s, Heyhoe Flint became involved in the campaign to elect women as Members of MCC, and in 1999, she became one of the first ten women Members. She had initially applied for MCC membership in 1990 under the name R. Flint. She was proposed and seconded by Jack Hayward and Tim Rice, making her the first woman to apply. However, her application was rejected at the time because one of MCC's officials recognised her address and flagged her sex. As a result of these events, MCC's Committee decided to ask the Members to vote on whether to accept women as Members. The initial vote to allow women Members was defeated, but change eventually occurred in 1999. Before that, with few exceptions, the Queen had been the only woman permitted in the Pavilion and on the field of play.

The first ten women elected as MCC Members are recognised here:

Betty Archdale – captain of the first women's cricket team to tour Australia and New Zealand in 1934/5.

Edna Barker – toured Australia and New Zealand with England, earning fifteen caps.

Audrey Collins – played cricket from the 1930s for over four decades. She was President of the Women's Cricket Association (WCA) from 1981–93.

Carole Cornthwaite – played eighteen Test matches for England, and captained the team in 1986 and 1987 in six Tests and five One Day Internationals.

Jackie Court – represented England forty times.

Rachael Heyhoe Flint – played for England from 1960–79. Captained England in twelve Tests and nine One Day Internationals.

Sheila Hill – played cricket for Oxford University, Kent and East England. She also umpired the first women's World Cup match between England and Australia.

Norma Izard – President of the WCA from 1994–98, and the longest-serving senior England manager with twelve international tours before stepping down in 1993.

Diana Rait Kerr – served as the first curator of MCC's Museum from 1945–68.

Netta Rheinberg – player/manager of the England tour to Australia and New Zealand in 1948/9. She was also secretary of the WCA in 1945, and from 1948–58.

Today, women cricketers are professionals with opportunities to play all around the world and to enjoy the celebrity status that goes with it. Arguably, this is Heyhoe Flint's most significant legacy.

To commemorate her life and achievements, the East Gate at Lord's was replaced with the Heyhoe Flint Gates. The official dedication ceremony was conducted by Heyhoe Flint's son, Ben, alongside MCC President Clare Connor and MCC's Chief Executive and Secretary, Guy Lavender. A bas-relief sculpture of Baroness Rachael Heyhoe Flint and a plaque were also unveiled.

Rachael Heyhoe Flint's initials on the gate. (JL)

5. Bicentenary Gates

Further along St John's Wood Road, heading towards the Grace Gates, are the MCC Bicentenary Gates. The Duke of Westminster presented these gates to MCC in honour of his uncle, Charles John Lyttelton, 10th Viscount Cobham, a former President of MCC. The gates were unveiled in May 1987 to commemorate the bicentenary of the club.

The inscription is indistinct and is reproduced here:

M.C.C. BICENTENARY GATES
Presented May 1987 by
The Duke of Westminster
in memory of his uncle
Charles Lyttelton 10TH Viscount Cobham
President M.C.C. 1955

Charles John Lyttelton, born in 1909 in Kensington, London, was a cousin of the jazz musician Humphrey Lyttelton. He received his education at Eton and Trinity College, Cambridge, qualifying as a lawyer before embarking on a military and diplomatic career, culminating in his tenure as Governor-General of New Zealand. Lyttelton was also a cricketer and made his debut for Worcestershire in June 1932. He played over ninety matches for his county during the 1930s, captaining the club from 1936 to 1939. He scored more than 3,000 first-class runs, with a highest score of 162 against Leicestershire in 1938.

Commemorating the presentation of the Bicentenary Gates. (JL)

As a former President of MCC, Lyttelton became involved in the D'Oliveira affair and had several discussions with the President of South Africa, John Vorster. During those meetings, Lyttelton was told 'quite categorically' that the selection of Basil D'Oliveira – a cricketer of 'Cape Coloured' origin – in MCC's team to tour South Africa that winter would not be acceptable to the South African government.

*The D'Oliveira Affair

Basil D'Oliveira was a talented all-round cricketer who played for Worcestershire and England during the 1960s and 1970s. Born in South Africa, he was classified as 'Cape Coloured' by the apartheid government there and, consequently, was ineligible to play first-class cricket in his country of birth.

With the assistance of writer and broadcaster John Arlott, D'Oliveira joined Middleton Cricket Club in the Central Lancashire Cricket League for the 1960 season. After a successful stint with Middleton, D'Oliveira became a Worcestershire player in 1964. He gained British nationality in 1965 and made his Test debut for England at Lord's in June 1966.

The 'affair' was sparked when the England team was scheduled to tour South Africa in the winter of 1968–69. Controversy arose over whether the England selectors would pick D'Oliveira in the team. However, during the 1968 English season, his form declined, and he was omitted from the England team but returned for the final Test against Australia at the Oval, where he scored 158. Despite this, he was excluded from the touring party. Days later, Tom Cartwright withdrew from the team and D'Oliveira was selected, much to the annoyance of the South African authorities. Due to the controversy surrounding these events, the tour was eventually cancelled on 24 September 1968.

These events significantly impacted South African cricket, leading to its isolation from international cricket. South Africa eventually rejoined the international cricket community in 1991.

6. Mound Stand Stone

Continuing along St John's Wood Road, a stone tablet is set into the exterior brickwork of Lord's Ground to commemorate the opening of the remodelled Mound Stand in 1987. As with the Bicentenary Gates, the opening of the new Mound Stand coincided with MCC's bicentenary.

When the Mound Stand was first developed in 1899 to replace the Real Tennis Court, the change was not well received. On 15 July 1899, *The Standard*, reporting on the Eton versus Harrow match, stated that 'Lord's of to-day is not the Lord's of a season ago'. The article continued, 'in place of the tented stands, the ivy-clad tennis court, and the bold array of carriages, which in the old days were an inseparable feature of the match, huge mounds of brick and mortar have been reared in their stead'.

Commemoration of the Mound Stand's redevelopment. (JL)

The stone's inscription reads:

THE NEW MOUND STAND
WAS OPENED ON 6TH MAY 1987 BY
H.R.H. THE PRINCE PHILIP
DUKE OF EDINBURGH, KG, KT.
PRESIDENT M.C.C. 1949 AND 1975

The redevelopment of the Mound Stand at Lord's, which included constructing the upper tier and installing its distinctive canopied roof, was a significant undertaking in the development of the Ground. The opening ceremony was conducted by HRH The Duke of Edinburgh*, a former MCC President, on 6 May 1987.

This plaque is situated outside the Ground, and its position only affords a view of the rear of the Mound Stand. From here, it is impossible to appreciate the splendour of the tented canopy, designed to remind visitors of village and country house cricket. The Mound Stand's brick arcade – designed by Frank Verity (son of Thomas Verity) in 1898 – has survived and has been extended to create an attractive public concourse behind the stand.

The redevelopment of the stand was made possible by a generous donation from Sir Paul Getty. A plaque recognising this is located on the stand itself (see Number 30). The stand was designed by Michael Hopkins, Architects, and was built at a cost of £4.35 million.

*HRH The Duke of Edinburgh

A lover of cricket, The Duke of Edinburgh served as President of MCC on two occasions: first in 1949 and again in 1975. He has officially opened five structures at Lord's Ground.

Starting with the Memorial Gallery (now the MCC's Museum) in 1953, he also opened the Mound Stand in 1987, the MCC's Indoor School in 1995, and the Grand Stand in 1998. Finally, as one of his last public engagements before retirement, he opened the new Warner Stand in 2017.

7. Grace Gates

One individual dominated cricket in the later Victorian era, a period often referred to as cricket's 'Golden Age'. That person was William Gilbert ('W. G.') Grace. He was a powerful force who aided in the transformation of the game from primarily a niche English pastime into the global sport it is today. His exploits at Lord's helped establish Thomas Lord's Ground as the spiritual and administrative 'Home of Cricket'.

When Grace died in 1915, there was a desire to ensure that his name and long association with the Club were commemorated forever at Lord's Ground. However, as *The Globe* reported on 14 December 1915:

> A council meeting of the M.C.C. was held at the Junior Carlton Club last night, Lord Hawke presiding. The committee had under discussion the question of a memorial to the late Dr. W. G. Grace, but no definite decision was arrived at, as it was thought the time was hardly opportune.

With the First World War still raging in Europe, any decision was delayed.

Thoughts of commissioning a Grace memorial were revived at the conclusion of hostilities in 1918. However, on this occasion, Frank Verity, the Club's preferred architect, was not chosen to design it. Verity's practice had suffered during the years of the Great War, culminating in bankruptcy in 1920. Instead, MCC asked Herbert Baker, an experienced architect who had worked extensively in South Africa and India, to design the memorial.

Initially, Baker proposed that a bust of Grace be placed on a plinth at the Nursery End of the Ground – a practice area since it had been purchased by MCC in 1887 – situated directly opposite the Pavilion. However, this suggestion did not gain the Committee's approval as it would have hindered the ground staff's ability to move equipment onto and off the Ground. After extensive further discussion, it was ultimately agreed that a memorial gateway into the Ground would be the most fitting monument to Grace.

The Grace Gates with the Tavern Stand in the background. (JL)

The design was approved in 1921, and the Gates were erected in the southern exterior wall on St John's Wood Road by June 1922. Flanked by walls and piers made of Portland stone, the gates are made of wrought iron and were produced by the Bromsgrove Guild, the company responsible for the gates at Buckingham Palace. The Grace Gates are topped with a decorative design of a cricket ball under a blazing sun, along with the initials MCC. On the central pillar is a carved wreath featuring the initials WGG. The memorial replaced an earlier, unattractive entrance to the ground and was officially unveiled by Sir Stanley Jackson*. Indeed, it was Jackson who had suggested including the words 'The Great Cricketer'.

The central, larger pillar carries this inscription:

TO THE
MEMORY OF
WILLIAM GILBERT
GRACE
THE GREAT CRICKETER
1848–1915:
THESE GATES WERE
ERECTED: THE MCC
AND OTHER FRIENDS
AND ADMIRERS

*Sir Stanley Jackson

Born in Yorkshire in 1870, Sir Francis Stanley Jackson was a cricketing contemporary of W. G. Grace. Between 1893 and 1905, Jackson played in twenty Test matches for England, including a match against Australia at the Oval in 1893 (below) where he is pictured on W. G. Grace's left.

Jackson attended Harrow School before enrolling at Trinity College, Cambridge, in 1889. During his time at Harrow, the future Prime Minister Winston Churchill was Jackson's 'fag'.

The England team at the Oval in August 1893. (MCC)

Jackson played cricket for Cambridge University, Yorkshire, and England. In 1894, he was named a *Wisden* Cricketer of the Year and became an Ashes-winning captain in 1905 when England won two of the five matches and drew the remaining three. He was also a member of the Yorkshire team that secured multiple county championships. Jackson served as MCC President in 1921 and, in 1938, succeeded Lord Hawke as President of the Yorkshire County Cricket Club following Hawke's death. Jackson remained in that role until his own death in 1947. He also had a lengthy political career and eventually became the Chairman of the Conservative Party.

The central column of the Grace Gates. (JL)

During the 1960s, a banqueting suite (now called the Thomas Lord Suite), a large block of flats named Century Court, and the Tavern Stand were constructed. This required moving the Grace Gates approximately 13 feet to the east. The Gates became a Grade II listed structure in 1996 and serve as the main entrance to Lord's for MCC Members. On major match days, MCC Members often queue for hours before the gates open to secure a prime seat, either in the Pavilion or in other Members' areas.

THE GARDENS

There are two formal garden areas at Lord's, both located behind the Pavilion. Upon entering the Ground through the Grace Gates, the first garden encountered is the Harris Garden. Formerly a lawn tennis court, this area is now used for socialising during major matches. Set into the wall towards the back of the garden is a stone tablet commemorating the life of Lord Harris and his contributions to cricket.

8. Harris Memorial Tablet

The creation of the Harris Garden celebrated Lord Harris's long relationship with MCC and Lord's Ground. After Harris's death in 1932, several proposals were evaluated to determine how to preserve his memory at Lord's. Ideas included a 'Wall of Honour' proposed for the Nursery End of the Ground, which would have featured bas-relief portraits of great players from the past. Additionally, a new gateway on St John's Wood Road was considered. However, MCC's Committee eventually decided on the Memorial we see today. The flint used in the wall's construction came from Harris's estate in Kent.

Commemorating Lord Harris's contribution to cricket. (JL)

An idea to create a niche to house a bust of Harris was rejected in favour of an inscribed tablet embedded in the wall, which states:

ERECTED TO THE MEMORY OF
GEORGE ROBERT CANNING
1851 LORD HARRIS 1932
BY THE MCC
IN RECOGNITION OF INVALUABLE SERVICES
RENDERED TO CRICKET AND TO THE CLUB OVER
A PERIOD OF MORE THAN FIFTY YEARS HE WAS
A GREAT CRICKETER A GREAT GENTLEMAN
AND A WISE COUNSELLOR WHOSE
ENTHUSIASM FOR THE GAME NEVER WANED

Beneath the inscribed tablet lies the primary location for the scattering of ashes of MCC Members and others, when permitted by MCC. In exceptional cases, ashes have also been scattered on the Lord's outfield, including the remains of Sir Pelham Warner, the actor Trevor Howard, Denis Compton, and Charles Fry (MCC's President in 2004).

Like W. G. Grace, George Robert Canning Harris (better known as Lord Harris) was one of the most influential figures in cricket during the late Victorian era and into the twentieth century, initially as a player and later as an administrator. In his youth, he was a talented batsman and an outstanding fielder, maintaining a commanding presence in cricket for the rest of his life.

Born in Trinidad in February 1851, Harris was educated at Eton and Oxford. Throughout his life, he maintained a close association with Kent County Cricket Club

Lord Harris in his playing days. (MCC)

and made his debut for the county in 1870 at the age of nineteen. He served Kent CCC in many capacities, including captain, committee member, honorary secretary, president, trustee, and chairman. Harris also played for and captained England in four Test matches, becoming the second England Test captain after James Lillywhite.

Harris was also a prominent politician, holding two senior roles – Under-Secretary of State for India and Under-Secretary of State for War in the Cabinets of the Marquess of Salisbury and William Gladstone, respectively.

Almost as close as the connection he had with Kent was his relationship with MCC. He was first elected to the Committee in 1875, became President of MCC in 1895, served as a Trustee from 1906 to 1916, and was Treasurer from 1916 until 1932. Additionally, he chaired both the MCC finance and cricket sub-committees, which gave him considerable influence in the world of cricket.

As well as being extremely influential, Harris could also be a controversial figure. He was responsible for omitting K. S. Ranjitsinhji (Ranji) from the England side for the Lord's Test in 1896, believing that an Indian cricketer should not play for England. Ranji was later selected by the authorities at Old Trafford and scored a century against Australia on his England debut. Additionally, Harris might have deprived England of the services of one of its greatest batsmen. Walter Hammond was born in Kent but chose to play for Gloucestershire in the early 1920s. Harris believed that since Hammond had not fulfilled the required period of residence to qualify for Gloucestershire, he should be barred from playing for them until the necessary time had elapsed. The Hammond incident resulted in Harris describing the 'bolshevism' that he felt was influencing cricket.

Unafraid to take on difficult challenges, Harris was also heavily involved in the campaign to outlaw 'throwing' – an illegal delivery by the bowler. In 1885, Harris advised Kent to refuse to play Lancashire due to their employment of 'unfair' bowlers.

Colonel George Robert Canning Harris, 4th Baron Harris, GCSI, GCIE, CB, TD, ADC, died on 24 March 1932, at the age of eighty-two.

9. Women's Ashes

Unveiled in 2023 and placed along the central path near the entrance to the Harris Garden, a simple plaque commemorates the creation of the Women's Ashes.

Since 1882, the original Ashes Urn, located in the MCC Museum, has symbolised the friendly rivalry between the English and Australian men's cricket teams. The image of an Ashes-winning captain holding a replica of the Urn at the end of a Test series has inspired many generations of cricketers.

Demand for a Women's Ashes began to grow, and on 20 July 1998, a brief ceremony took place in the Harris Garden at Lord's Cricket Ground, attended by around thirty people, including the England and Australia women players. They were scheduled to play each other in a One Day International the following day.

Norma Izard, OBE, the President of the Women's Cricket Association (WCA) and former England women's manager, conceived the idea and designed the Ashes trophy. Izard commissioned a woodcarver to create a hollow cricket ball from wood sourced from a 300-year-old yew tree. She also acquired a miniature cricket bat signed by both teams. Along with a copy of the WCA constitution, the miniature bat was placed in a large wok borrowed from the kitchens at Lord's. The items were then burned, and the ashes were placed into the hollow wooden ball, forming the Women's Ashes.

Later that year, the WCA, the organisation that had governed women's cricket in Britain for seventy-two years, merged with the England and Wales Cricket Board (ECB), creating a unified governing body for both the men's and women's games. This significant event occurred sixty-four years after the first-ever women's Test match between England and Australia, which was played in Australia in 1934–35.

In 2023, to mark the twenty-fifth anniversary of the creation of the Women's Ashes, guests gathered for the unveiling of a plaque to commemorate that moment. Among

Right: Plaque marking the creation of the Women's Ashes in 1998. (JL)

Below: Unveiling the Women's Ashes plaque. (MCC and JL)

those present were players who attended the original ceremony, including former MCC President Clare Connor. The plaque was unveiled by MCC's President at the time, Stephen Fry. It was a fitting event to honour an important moment in women's cricket.

10. W. G. Grace Statue

Behind the Pavilion, near the Warner Stand, is the Coronation Garden, which was established in 1953 to commemorate the Coronation of Queen Elizabeth II. On major match days, the garden is adorned with picnic blankets and hampers, making it a popular gathering point for MCC Members and their friends.

The tenth item in this series is located towards the rear of the grassed area. It is a larger-than-life-sized statue of a towering figure in the world of cricket – William Gilbert Grace MRCS LRCP, better known as W. G. Grace. Created by Australian sculptor Louis Laumen, the statue was initially exhibited at Gloucestershire County Cricket Club's Ground in Bristol (Grace's home county) from 12 May 2000. Later, it was brought to Lord's Ground for display and subsequently purchased by MCC for permanent exhibition.

W. G. Grace dominated the Victorian cricketing world for over forty years. He was an amateur cricketer who significantly influenced the sport's development and became one of its greatest players. Grace was known for his competitive attitude and, through cricket, became one of the most famous individuals in the country, while also being one of the most controversial figures due to his moneymaking activities and gamesmanship.

Laumen's statue of W. G. Grace in Coronation Garden. (JL)

Formative Years – 1848–69

Born in Bristol on 14 July 1848, W. G. Grace came from a large cricketing family. He was the eighth of nine siblings. Edward Mills (E. M.) Grace was one of his three older brothers, and George Frederick (G. F.) Grace was his younger brother. Better known as Fred, G. F. was the youngest of the Grace siblings, born in 1850.

Grace was fifteen years old at the start of the 1864 season and twenty years old at the climax of the 1868 season. In those four short years, Grace came to be regarded as the country's finest cricketer and the sport's foremost attraction. During this period, cricket was the leading spectator sport in a time that coincided with the establishment of the Football Association in 1863.

Grace was not academically gifted but was encouraged by his father to pursue a medical career. His prowess in cricket attracted offers from clubs at both Oxford and Cambridge universities. However, in October 1868, Grace chose to enrol at Bristol Medical School, eventually qualifying as a doctor. His later medical work included establishing his own practice in Easton, one of Bristol's poorer areas, where he also served as the local public vaccinator. Grace employed two locums during the cricket season to allow him to continue his cricket career.

W. G. Grace became an MCC Member in 1869 at the age of twenty-one. He was proposed by Thomas Burgoyne, MCC's Treasurer, and seconded by Robert Allan Fitzgerald, the Secretary of MCC. From that point on, Grace consistently wore MCC's colours. He played for the club until 1904.

Grace's Peak – 1870–95

In 1870, Gloucestershire attained first-class county status. Around that time, Grace began to grow his large black beard. At a time when most cricketers favoured extravagant moustaches, this choice, combined with his height of around 6 feet 3 inches, his MCC cap, and his build, made him stand out even more. By the time he was in his early twenties, Grace had developed a generous waistline, weighing nearly 15 stone, largely due to his enjoyment of good food and wine.

The year 1871 was a defining one for Grace. He scored ten first-class centuries, averaging just over seventy-eight, and accumulated a total of 2,739 runs that season. However, the year was also tinged with sadness as his father, Henry Grace, died in December at the age of sixty-three. The *Gloucestershire Chronicle* of 30 December 1871 described Henry Grace as 'beloved for his professional kindness towards the poor'. This quality was also noted during W. G.'s medical career.

During this golden period, Grace was responsible for several 'firsts' in domestic cricket. In 1873, he became the first batsman to score 100 before lunch in a first-class match, and in the same year, he was the first cricketer to complete the 'double' of 1,000 runs and 100 wickets in a season, a feat he accomplished eight times during his career.

In May 1895, he scored his hundredth century, finishing on 288 in the Gloucestershire versus Somerset match. After that match, Gloucestershire supporters organised a celebratory dinner for Grace. According to another guest, 'He drank something of everything, before and during dinner, and afterwards he sent for the whisky. You couldn't make the Old Man drunk.' Grace went on to score 1,000 runs before the end of May – the first time that had been done. That total included one other double hundred.

Australian captain Billy Murdoch and W. G. Grace in 1890. (MCC)

Financial Matters and Disputes

In 1878, tension arose between Grace and several members of the touring Australian cricket team, a situation exacerbated by a dispute regarding the status of the Australian player and Grace's friend Billy Midwinter. Midwinter had played for Gloucestershire in 1877 and was already in England before the Australian touring party arrived. He joined Australia for their first match and, in late June, was selected to play for Australia against Middlesex at Lord's. Grace and his Gloucestershire team were at the Oval in South London, scheduled to play Surrey on the same day. Gloucestershire arrived one man short, prompting a group of their players – led by the Grace brothers, W. G. and E. M. – to head to Lord's to persuade Midwinter to join them at the Oval. Several furious Australian players followed the group to the Oval, leading to an altercation. Ultimately, the Grace brothers prevailed, and Midwinter played for, and then stayed with, Gloucestershire for the remainder of the season.

In January 1879, due to those events at the Oval, W. G. and E. M. were asked by Gloucestershire members to account for the expenses claimed from Surrey for that match, which Surrey had refused to authorise. It was suggested that the expenses claim submitted by the brothers had been excessive. The Grace brothers survived this episode and agreed to abide by stricter rules in the future.

Like many amateur* cricketers, the Grace brothers claimed travel and accommodation expenses related to their cricketing activities. Grace also received two testimonials. The first, at Lord's in July 1879, included a cheque for £1,458 – equivalent to around £180,000 in today's terms. The second, organised by MCC, Gloucestershire CCC, *The Daily Telegraph*, and *The Sportsman* magazine, raised £9,703 (equivalent to £1.3 million today). This was presented to him in 1896, the year following his 'Indian Summer' season of 1895. In the late 1890s, W. G. also received a salary as secretary and manager of the short-lived London County Cricket Club.

*Amateurs and Professionals

In its formative years, cricket was a game enjoyed by everyone. As the game developed, amateur clubs like the White Conduit Club began to employ professional players, including Thomas Lord. A clear distinction emerged between amateurs (Gentlemen) and professionals (Players), although the reality was that many leading amateurs were, in fact, compensated for playing.

Change occurred at the end of the Second World War, and the distinction between amateurs and professionals began to fade. However, one tradition persisted, with the last Gentlemen v Players fixture being played in Scarborough in September 1962.

Fred Titmus, a distinguished player for Middlesex and England from the 1950s until the 1970s, was a professional cricketer during the era when amateurs were noted in scorecards with their initials before their surname, and professionals with their initials after their surname. On one occasion, Titmus came out to bat for Middlesex at Lord's, and a loudspeaker announcement informed the spectators that they should amend one entry on the scorecard – 'For F. J. Titmus, please read Titmus, F. J.'.

Despite some criticism levelled at Grace for profiting from cricket, he was consistently generous in helping professional players when they were awarded benefit matches by their counties. There are instances of Grace donating to players' benefits when, for example, their matches were ruined by weather. On one occasion, Grace even changed the date of a Gloucestershire match he was scheduled to play in to travel to Yorkshire and participate in a player's benefit match. He understood that his appearance would positively influence ticket sales.

In the late 1890s, Grace was playing at Leyton for Gloucestershire against Essex, which featured a player widely recognised as the country's fastest bowler, Charles Kortright. A large crowd had gathered to witness this confrontation. Ill feelings arose on the first morning when Grace successfully appealed for a catch to dismiss Percy Perrin. It was clear to all that Grace had taken the catch after the ball had bounced.

Charles Kortright of Essex. (MCC)

On the morning of the second day, Essex's Bunny Lucas was given out caught after the ball had clearly brushed his shirt. Lucas returned to the pavilion, shouting to the angry crowd 'Cheats never prosper'. As day two ended, Grace persuaded umpire George Burton to reverse a decision when he was clearly out caught and bowled. Kortright and the rest of the Essex team were furious. Kortright bowled the next over which included some ferocious short-pitched deliveries, leaving Grace bruised. One of these deliveries resulted in Grace offering up a difficult catch, which an Essex fielder dropped. Kortright expressed his displeasure when the players left the field of play. On hearing this, Grace added fuel to the flames by repeating Lucas's earlier comment, 'Cheats never prosper'.

Day three brought more controversy. Kortright was convinced that he had dismissed Grace in two consecutive deliveries: first, through an unsuccessful appeal for leg before wicket, and then by being caught behind the wicket. Again, Grace persuaded umpire Burton that he was 'not out'. The third delivery from a furious Kortright saw Grace's middle stump cartwheeling out of the ground, also knocking back the leg stump. As Grace left the field, Kortright apparently said to him, 'Surely you're not going Doc, there's still one stump standing.' Later, Grace said that he had never been so insulted in his life. The pair made peace soon after when they were both selected to play for the

Gentlemen against the Players. The Gentlemen lost the match, but Kortright and Grace were batting together at the end, linking arms to leave the ground to the cheers of the crowd.

George Burton, the umpire in that difficult match, was a seasoned cricketer but lacked experience as an umpire. Indeed, this was just his fifth match in charge, and he ceased officiating after six more matches. At that time, it was common for former professional players to take up umpiring as a way to earn some money in retirement, and some were intimidated by well-known and influential amateur players like W. G. Grace. Only the bravest umpires would have had the confidence to confront Grace's bullying.

Test Cricket

Between 1877 and 1894, matches between countries were simply known as international matches. Thirty-nine matches played during that period were retrospectively given Test match status. Grace made his England Test debut in September 1880 at the Oval in South London – the first Test match played on English soil. During this match against Australia, he scored England's first Test century. This hastily arranged three-day match between a representative England XI and the visiting Australians was also notable because three Grace brothers – Fred, E. M., and W. G. – all played in the same England team, marking the first time this had occurred.

Nearly 21,000 spectators attended on the first day, and around 20,000 on the second day. Vantage points around the ground – including the gasometers – were also fully occupied. W. G. batted for almost four hours and amassed 152 runs. This exciting game concluded on the third day with an England win by five wickets. However, there was a sad postscript to this match. At the conclusion of the game, Fred Grace left the Oval to travel to Stroud in Gloucestershire. Heavy rain fell throughout his journey, and he became thoroughly soaked. He then spent the night sleeping on a damp mattress, which resulted in him catching pneumonia. Two weeks later, Fred died.

The 1882 match at the Oval was significant as it sparked the creation of 'the Ashes'. It is estimated that around 20,000 spectators were present on each of the two days. Contemporary reports stated that the crowd was standing sixty deep around the ground. The match was a tense, low-scoring, rain-affected, and quite bad-tempered affair, dominated by the Australian bowler Frederick Spofforth – known as the 'Demon Bowler' – who took fourteen wickets in the match. On day two, the England team was set eighty-five runs to win but was bowled out for seventy-seven, losing by seven runs. A subsequent mock obituary lamenting 'the death of English Cricket' in the *Sporting Times* magazine contained the first mention of the Ashes. Although Grace contributed little to the match, he was thought to have fired up Spofforth by effecting a legal, although possibly unsporting, run out of an Australian player.

Grace's last match for England was the first Test of the 1899 Australia series. At the age of fifty-one, he had become a liability as a fielder. Grace later reflected on his decision, saying, 'the ground was getting a bit too far away'.

Batting, Bowling, Fielding and Captaincy

Sir Pelham Warner described Grace's batting style, writing that he had 'revolutionised the art of batting and made modern cricket. Before his day, a batsman was either a back player or a forward player, "W. G." combined both styles.' One of Grace's contemporaries, K. S. Ranjitsinhji, claimed that 'the theory of modern batting is in all essentials the result of W. G.'s thinking and working on the game'.

Grace's bowling action was essentially roundarm, yet he maintained a consistent length. In his younger days, he bowled at a fast-medium pace. In the 1870s, he adopted a slower style using leg breaks. He continued with a roundarm action throughout his career, even though the overarm action had been legalised in 1864.

Grace was widely recognised as an exceptional fielder and was reputed to have thrown a cricket ball 122 yards during an athletics event held in Eastbourne. He once claimed that he had developed this ability by throwing stones at crows during his childhood in the countryside.

Due to his immense ability and force of personality, W. G. Grace often captained most of the teams for which he played. Throughout his career, it was evident that as captain, Grace could not tolerate slackness in any of his teams, and he was viewed as a disciplinarian. More information on W. G. Grace and his legacy can be found in a later section (see Number 16).

Later Years

After his international career ended, Grace joined the newly formed London County Cricket Club (LCCC) at Crystal Palace Park. The LCCC played first-class matches between 1900 and 1904. Despite its initial success and the addition of other famous players like C. B. Fry and K. S. Ranjitsinhji, the club could not compete with the growing importance of the County Championship. This led to smaller attendances and financial losses. The LCCC folded in 1908.

In retirement, Grace and his family moved to Mottingham in Kent. He developed a keen interest in bowls, curling, and golf. Bernard Darwin – a biographer of Grace – said that Grace played golf 'with a mixture of keen seriousness and cheerful noisiness'.

In August 1914, following the outbreak of the First World War, Grace wrote to *The Sportsman* magazine, calling for county cricket to be suspended. He believed that first-class cricketers should set an example and serve their country. Grace was known to shake his fist and shout at the German Zeppelins that passed over his South London home. He died on 23 October 1915, at the age of sixty-seven, following a heart attack, and is buried in the family grave at Beckenham Cemetery in Kent.

11. Keith Miller Tree

Behind the Warner Stand and positioned against the perimeter wall is a eucalyptus tree planted during the Ashes Test match in 2005 by MCC President Tom Graveney, in memory of one of the finest cricketers to ever play the game. Keith Miller, an esteemed Australian cricketer known as the 'Golden Nugget', was one of the leading all-rounders of his era, and his exploits are still highly regarded to this day.

Eucalyptus tree planted in memory of Keith Miller. (JL)

The inscription reads:

Eucalyptus pauciflora ssp. Niphophila
"Snow Gun"

In Memory of
K. R. Miller M.B.E.
1919 – 2004
M.C.C. Member 1959 to 2004
Who represented Australia in 55 Test Matches

Miller served in the Second World War, flying Mosquito fighter-bombers in combat. In the spring and early summer of 1945, Miller's squadron was tasked with attacking targets in mainland Europe, specifically the V-1 flying bomb and the V-2 rocket launch sites. His wartime experiences highlighted the relatively unimportant nature of playing cricket compared to deadly combat, reinforcing the swashbuckling approach to the game for which he was renowned. In his later years, Miller was asked by television chat show host Michael Parkinson about the pressure of playing cricket. Miller responded, 'Pressure, I'll tell you what pressure is. Pressure is a Messerschmitt up your arse, playing is not.'

Miller's cricket career took off after the war with memorable appearances in the 'Victory Tests' – three of which were at Lord's. These were matches organised for the English and Australian Services teams during the summer of 1945. Although not truly representative, some notable cricketers, including Lindsay Hassett and Walter

Hammond, participated. That summer, he also played for the Dominions against England, scoring 185 in under three hours, which included seven sixes and thirteen fours.

In the post-war period, Miller formed an effective opening bowling partnership with Ray Lindwall. He played in fifty-five Test matches for Australia, scoring 2,958 runs at an average of just under thirty-seven. This total included seven centuries and a top score of 147. He also took 177 Test wickets, with an impressive average of 22.

Miller played in three Ashes Test matches at Lord's during the post-war period, starting in 1948 (as part of Don Bradman's 'Invincibles'), then in 1953 and again in 1956. He is one of a select group of three visiting cricketers to feature on both the batting and bowling sides of the Test match Honours Boards in the Visitors' Dressing Room at Lord's, the others being Garfield Sobers and Vinoo Mankad.

Keith Miller shared a strong friendship with Denis Compton after meeting him during the Second World War in India. In 2005, the Compton–Miller Medal was inaugurated as an award for the Player of the Series in an individual Ashes series between Australia and England.

THE PAVILION'S EXTERIOR

12. Pavilion Foundation Stone

The Foundation Stone is situated on the external southeastern wall of the Pavilion, outside the Committee Room and in the space between the Allen Stand and the Pavilion. It was laid on 17 September 1889 by Sir Spencer Ponsonby-Fane, marking the beginning of the Pavilion's construction, which was designed by Thomas Verity*.

*Thomas Verity

Born in 1837, Thomas Verity was a prominent British architect renowned for designing several of London's theatres constructed in the late nineteenth and early twentieth centuries.

Verity began his career in the architecture department of the War Office, assisting in the design and construction of prominent London buildings, including the South Kensington Museum (now the Victoria and Albert Museum) and the Royal Albert Hall.

He established his own practice in 1870, and in the same year, he was awarded a commission to build the Criterion Theatre and Criterion Restaurant in Piccadilly Circus. He was also responsible for the Royalty Theatre, Novelty Theatre, Folly Theatre, Scala Theatre, and Comedy Theatre. Thomas Verity initially collaborated with G. H. Hunt but later teamed up with his son, Frank.

Many of Verity's buildings have been recognised for their architectural significance in the late twentieth century, with some achieving listed building status, including the Lord's Pavilion.

Following the death of Thomas Verity in 1891, Frank Verity continued the architectural practice. In the 1920s, he was joined by his son-in-law, Sam Beverley, and the practice remains active today.

The inscription on the stone reads:

THIS STONE WAS LAID
BY THE HONBLE
SIR SPENCER PONSONBY FANE K.C.B.
TREASURER OF THE M.C.C.
17th SEPTEMBER 1899.
T. VERITY J. SIMPSON & SON
ARCHITECT BUILDERS

Pavilion Foundation Stone laid in September 1899. (JL)

Ponsonby-Fane was a cricketer who represented both Middlesex and Surrey. Later, he became involved in the administration of Somerset County Cricket Club and Harrow Cricket Club. Ponsonby-Fane had many long-standing connections with Lord's. His uncle by marriage, the Reverend Lord Frederick Beauclerk, played in the first-ever match at Lord's third Ground in June 1814 against Hertfordshire.

In 1845, Ponsonby-Fane was one of the founders of I Zingari* ('The Gypsies' in Italian), a wandering cricket club. He served as the MCC's Treasurer from 1879 and played a crucial role in establishing the MCC's collection of cricketing and other artefacts. Ponsonby-Fane was also involved in government, holding several key positions in the Foreign Office.

*I Zingari

On 4 July 1845, a group of Old Harrovians – the Hon. Spencer Ponsonby (later, Sir Spencer Ponsonby-Fane), John Loraine Baldwin, William Bolland, the Hon. Frederick Ponsonby (later, 6th Earl of Bessborough), Richard Penruddocke Long, and Edward Dewing – met for dinner at the Blenheim Hotel in Bond Street and decided to form a cricket club to maintain the spirit of amateur cricket. Richard Long drifted off to sleep during the dinner, but awoke when the conversation turned to a name for this fledgling club. 'The Zingari, of course,' he said. By the morning, this had become 'I Zingari'.

Still active today, I Zingari is undoubtedly the oldest and perhaps the best-known 'wandering' cricket club. Renowned for its aristocratic membership, its colours – black, red, and gold – represent the club's motto, 'out of darkness, through fire, into light'. It is thought that the I Zingari colours may have inspired MCC to adopt the 'bacon and egg' colours in 1860, one of several theories.

Ponsonby-Fane was offered the presidency of MCC on several occasions but always declined. At the time of his death in 1915, he had been an MCC Member for seventy-five years.

13. Pavilion Refurbishment

Located directly below the original Foundation Stone is another commemoration stone that marks the refurbishment of and improvements to the Lord's Pavilion in the early 2000s, particularly noting the contribution made by Maurice de Rohan.

Maurice de Rohan was born in Adelaide, Australia, in 1936. He graduated from the University of Adelaide in 1960 with a civil engineering degree. In 1959, he founded Kinnaird, Hill, de Rohan and Young, which rapidly expanded throughout Australia, becoming one of the country's largest engineering and planning consultancies. In 1976, his firm's connections with Llewellyn-Davies Weeks International brought de Rohan to London.

Some ten years later, de Rohan lost his daughter and son-in-law in tragic circumstances. Both were victims of the 1987 Zeebrugge ferry disaster when the *Herald of Free Enterprise* car ferry capsized, resulting in the loss of 193 lives. In the aftermath, he played a significant role in establishing the Herald Families' Association, which sought justice for the victims and promoted the need for higher safety standards in the ferry industry. For his efforts in founding this Association, de Rohan was appointed an Officer of the Order of the British Empire (OBE) in the 1992 Queen's Birthday Honours List.

In 1986, de Rohan became an MCC Member, and he later chaired the estates committee for seven years. He was actively involved in a continuing development programme at the Ground that enhanced facilities for spectators, officials, and players. His most notable achievement was the £8 million refurbishment of Verity's Victorian

Commemorating the Pavilion's 2004/05 refurbishment. (JL)

Pavilion, completed in time for the 2006 season. This achievement is reflected in the stone, which reads:

THIS STONE IS DEDICATED
TO THE MEMORY OF
M. J. DE ROHAN. ESQ., A.O., O.B.E. [1936 – 2006]
CHAIRMAN OF ESTATES OF M.C.C.
AND MARKS HIS SIGNIFICANT INVOLVEMENT
IN THE RESTORATION OF THE PAVILION
DURING 2004 AND 2005

14. Second World War RAF Memorial

In early 1939, MCC's Secretary, Colonel Rowan Scrope Rait Kerr*, received an initial request from the United Kingdom Government for permission to use Lord's Ground in the event of war. In September of that year – eight days after the declaration of war on Germany – the MCC Committee, which by then had been renamed the 'Emergency Committee', met to discuss the impact of the outbreak of war on MCC and Lord's Ground.

*Colonel Rowan Scrope Rait Kerr DSO, MC

Born in Bray, Ireland, in April 1891, Colonel Rowan Scrope Rait Kerr served as MCC's Secretary from 1936, when he succeeded William Findlay, until his retirement in 1952. His tenure coincided with preparations for the Second World War and the challenges that followed in its aftermath.

Educated at Rugby School, Rait Kerr had a distinguished military career. After graduating from Sandhurst, he joined the Royal Engineers, and by 1916, at the age of twenty-five, he had been promoted to the rank of captain. He was subsequently promoted to the rank of acting major. His war service earned him both the Military Cross (MC) and the Distinguished Service Order (DSO).

He played a handful of first-class cricket matches, with the last being for the Army against Oxford University in 1931 when he was forty. Rait Kerr's daughter, Diana, became the first Curator of MCC's collection and was one of the first women elected to membership of MCC in 1999. Rait Kerr died at Constantine Bay in Cornwall in April 1961 at the age of sixty-nine.

By the end of 1939, the Pavilion's windows had been blacked out, all seats removed, and air raid shelters installed. The MCC's collection of books and paintings was moved to the Pavilion's basement for safekeeping. The collection was later transferred to two houses near Bletchley, Buckinghamshire, for storage.

During the war, Lord's Ground was affected by enemy bombing. In 1940, incendiary bombs caused damage to the Secretary's house, the roof of the Pavilion, and the Grand Stand. However, Lord's avoided significant damage despite the extensive bombing in the St John's Wood area.

In 1941, the Royal Air Force requisitioned the Ground, and for the remainder of the war, it served as a recruiting depot for young men joining the RAF as aircrew. This became known as the Air Crew Receiving Centre, later renamed No. 3 Air Crew Reception Centre (ACRC). After recruits passed selection boards elsewhere, they spent the next three to six weeks undergoing document checks, medical examinations, aptitude testing, and general service training. Between 1941 and 1944, 115,000 civilians and 44,000 military personnel passed through Lord's.

A small plaque was added to the rear of the Pavilion in 1992. Positioned approximately 30 yards to the right of the main entrance doors, the plaque commemorates the role of Lord's Cricket Ground during the Second World War, particularly its function as a recruiting depot for the Royal Air Force.

Remembering the role of Lord's during the Second World War. (JL)

MCC MUSEUM

The MCC Museum is situated directly behind the Pavilion at Lord's and is dedicated to collecting, preserving, documenting, and exhibiting cricket's history and development. It is one of the world's oldest sporting museums, housing the most extensive collection of cricket-related materials anywhere.

Origins (1864–1953)
MCC's collection began in 1864 when Members were invited to donate items of interest to furnish the Pavilion. For many years, the collection was accessible only to MCC Members, club officials, and players, as it was displayed in the Pavilion. Even the Ashes Urn, which arrived at Lord's in 1928, was initially placed in the Long Room. It became available for general viewing only when it was moved to the current Museum building in 1953.

By the end of the Second World War, attitudes were changing. The MCC's collection had outgrown the Pavilion, and following the cessation of hostilities in 1945, a new egalitarian spirit emerged. That year, MCC appointed its first Curator of Collections, Diana Rait Kerr, the daughter of Colonel Rowan Scrope Rait Kerr, a woman of remarkable gifts and determination. She was tasked with establishing a new Museum at the Ground where cricket supporters could learn about and appreciate the game's heritage. The chosen site was a disused racquets court at the rear of the Pavilion, which had fallen into disrepair during the war years. This building would also honour cricketers of all nations who had fallen during the two world wars and would be named the Imperial Cricket Memorial Gallery.

Rait Kerr exhibited tremendous energy, securing donations of pictures, equipment, and other artefacts from players and cricketing authorities around the world. She oversaw the fitting out of the new Gallery, which was completed in time for the scheduled opening on 27 April 1953. Fittingly, in what was Queen Elizabeth II's coronation year and with the Gallery situated adjacent to the new Coronation Garden, the formal opening was conducted by HRH The Duke of Edinburgh.

1953 to Date
From these modest beginnings, MCC's collection has significantly expanded and is now housed in the current Museum building, throughout the Pavilion, and in the extensive library. The Museum continually enhances its collection through loans, donations, bequests, purchases, and commissions. The generosity of players, administrators, and Members ensures that the Museum remains relevant and up to date.

The focal point of MCC's collection is the Ashes Urn – a personal gift from Lady Clarke in Melbourne to the England captain, the Hon. Ivo Bligh, during the 1882–83 England tour to Australia. It was later donated to MCC by his widow in 1928. The Museum also houses the first men's Cricket World Cup trophy and the balls used by Bob Massie to take sixteen wickets in the Lord's Ashes Test match in 1972. There is even an example of the taxidermist's art – an unfortunate sparrow that was killed by a cricket ball bowled by Jehangir Khan to Tom Pearce in a match at Lord's in 1936 (see Number 24).

15. Museum Opening Tablet

The stone tablet located just inside the Museum entrance and above the Ashes Urn was unveiled by HRH The Duke of Edinburgh on 27 April 1953 to officially open the Imperial Cricket Memorial Gallery. The ceremony was attended by a distinguished gathering of high commissioners, renowned cricketers past and present, and the Australian team, who had recently arrived for the 1953 Ashes series. The tablet includes a quotation from the American poet James Russell Lowell, which was chosen by the Hon. Charles Lyttelton, MCC's President in 1955, although this is shown as 1954 on the President's Boards in the Pavilion (see no. 39).

The tablet reads:

TO THE MEMORY OF CRICKETERS
OF ALL LANDS WHO GAVE THEIR
LIVES IN THE CAUSE OF FREEDOM
1914 – 1918 * 1939 - 1945

SECURE FROM CHANGE IN
THEIR HIGH-HEARTED WAYS

Tablet unveiled by The Duke of Edinburgh in 1953. (JL)

The Lowell quote 'Secure from change in their high-hearted ways' is also inscribed on the war memorial for cricketers who were not MCC Members (see Number 44).

Lord's Cricket Ground attracts around 500,000 visitors each year from cricket-playing countries and beyond. They primarily come to watch cricket, but about 70,000 of them also visit the MCC Museum and take part in guided tours. Alongside the many spectacular exhibits that showcase the evolution of cricket over the past 250 years, the MCC Museum has hosted various exhibitions, including cricket's connections with baseball, the history of black English cricketers, the history of women's cricket, and more.

16. Bust of W. G. Grace

To the left of the staircase in the Museum stands a plaster of Paris bust of W. G. Grace. This bust was created in 1888 by William Tyler when Grace was forty years old, and was donated to MCC by Grace's widow in 1919.

In 2019, Gloucestershire County Cricket Club received permission from MCC to create its own version of this original. In September 2021, they unveiled a bronze recast that cost £15,000 and is now on display at the Gloucestershire County Ground in Bristol.

Grace's Legacy

W. G. Grace's statistical achievements are secondary compared to his influence on cricket and his impact on the national consciousness. He was the outstanding cricketing and sporting figure for most of his life and was probably the most recognisable person in the country (apart from Queen Victoria) for many years.

Following his death, MCC commemorated Grace's life and career with a Memorial Biography, published in 1919. The installation of the Grace Memorial Gates followed in 1922.

Grace acquired various nicknames during his career, notably 'The Champion', 'The Great Cricketer', 'The Doctor', and later in his career, 'The Old Man'. He was also a pioneer in sports marketing, being the first sportsman to allow his image to be used

William Tyler's bust of W. G. Grace, dating from 1888. (JL)

for commercial purposes. For several years, his distinctive look was used to promote Colman's Mustard.

In the 1963 edition of *Wisden Cricketers' Almanack*, Neville Cardus selected Grace as one of the 'Six Giants of the Wisden Century'. The others chosen were Sydney Barnes, Don Bradman, Jack Hobbs, Tom Richardson, and Victor Trumper – exalted company indeed. In 1973, Grace appeared on commemorative British postage stamps celebrating the centenary of county cricket. Additionally, the Monty Python team in their 1975 film *Monty Python and the Holy Grail* used Grace's image as the face of God in the scene where God sends the knights out on their quest for the Grail.

More details on W. G. Grace and his life in cricket can be found in number 7 (Grace Gates) and number 10 (W. G. Grace Statue).

17. Bust of Benjamin Aislabie

To the right of the staircase in the MCC Museum stands a bust of Benjamin Aislabie, MCC's first Honorary Secretary. Born in London on 14 January 1774, Aislabie was the son of an English wine merchant and plantation owner. He became an MCC Member in 1802, and after his father's death in 1806, he inherited the family's plantations in Dominica, along with approximately £60,000 (equivalent to £1.5 million today).

Aislabie played cricket as a keen amateur, but did not distinguish himself on the field. Despite playing in over fifty first-class matches, he only averaged just over three runs per innings – statistically, one of the worst first-class cricketers ever to play the game. In 1883, the *Cricket* newspaper wrote about a match in 1827 at Lord's where:

> Aislabie greatly distinguished himself in this match, scoring 11 (not out) and 18. This was an unprecedented feat in the career of the worst cricketer who ever played in great matches. He was fifty-three at the time and portentously fat, but his cricket career continued till 1841.

Bust of Benjamin Aislabie, MCC's first Honorary Secretary. (JL)

In 1823, Aislabie became the Club's President and also served as its first Honorary Secretary from 1822 until his death in 1842. As Secretary of MCC, Aislabie laid the Foundation Stone of the first Real Tennis Court at Lord's on 15 October 1838 – a site now occupied by the Mound Stand. During his tenure, Aislabie attempted to reduce the widespread practice of gambling that was prevalent in the sport. He was recognised as a dedicated Honorary Secretary and, during the twenty years he served as Honorary Secretary, the Club's membership doubled from 200 to nearly 400. Aislabie was also a very popular after-dinner speaker, composing and performing his own cricket-themed songs at several MCC Anniversary dinners.

Like his father, Aislabie was a successful wine merchant and even supplied wine to Lord Nelson. In addition to the plantations in Dominica, he also owned several in Antigua. These estates utilised slave labour, and following the abolition of slavery in 1834, Aislabie received compensation for the loss of his slaves.

In 1838, MCC commissioned this bust of Aislabie, along with a portrait intended to hang in the Pavilion. MCC also holds William Novice's 1814 portrait of a younger Benjamin Aislabie. All three items remain at Lord's, although only the bust is on display. The paintings may be exhibited again in the future.

Aislabie died in London in 1842 at the age of sixty-eight and is buried at St Marylebone Parish Church.

18. Altham Memorial Tablet

Positioned on the wall halfway up the Museum's stairs is a fragment of the original tombstone of the Ground's founder, Thomas Lord. Known as the Altham Memorial Tablet, this stone was placed in the Museum in memory of Harry Surtees Altham, CBE, DSO, MC, a significant figure in cricket history. Altham was an administrator, coach, and respected historian. Born in 1888, he was educated at Repton School and Trinity College, Oxford. He had a distinguished military career during the First World War, for which he received the Distinguished Service Order (DSO) and the Military Cross (MC). He was also mentioned in dispatches three times.

Altham's involvement with Lord's included a long period on the MCC Committee, from 1941 until his death in 1965. He served as MCC's Treasurer between 1949 and 1963 and was the Club's President in 1959. Altham was also a prolific writer on cricket. His *History of Cricket* was first published in 1926, having started as a series of articles in *The Cricketer* magazine. He was actively involved with Hampshire CCC and served as Chairman of the England Test selection panel in 1954. When he died on 11 March 1965, his obituary in *Wisden* described him as one of 'the best-known personalities in the world of cricket'.

Following his death, the MCC Committee decided to commemorate Altham's contributions to both MCC and cricket. In April 1966, a proposal was made for a new library, along with the addition of a sundial or a drinking fountain to be placed in Coronation Garden. Finally, at an MCC sub-committee meeting on 2 April 1970, it was agreed that a plaque would be installed in the Memorial Gallery with the following wording:

HARRY SURTEES ALTHAM
1888 – 1965
PRESIDENT AND TREASURER OF M.C.C.
HE SERVED THE GAME WITH
DISTINCTION AS HISTORIAN,
ADMINISTRATOR, PLAYER AND COACH
AND CONCERNED HIMSELF ESPECIALLY
WITH YOUNG CRICKETERS FOR WHOM
A BURSARY HAS BEEN ENDOWED
WHICH BEARS HIS NAME.
HUMANITAS SEDULITAS AUCTORITAS

The sub-committee was not unanimous regarding the inclusion of a Latin inscription (meaning Humanity, Application, Authority). However, that was the wish of Mrs Altham and her family. At the same meeting, it was confirmed that Peter Wheble – a stonemason in Winchester and a long-standing friend of Harry Altham – would be able to use some of the Portland stone left over after the 1951 renovation of Thomas Lord's grave in West Meon.

Right: The Altham Memorial Tablet. (JL)

Below: Stone referring to the Altham Memorial Tablet. (JL)

On 26 May 1971, Altham's widow, their son, and MCC's President Sir Cyril Hawker unveiled the Altham Memorial Tablet. Later that same year, an additional stone plaque was added at floor level – again supplied by Peter Wheble – to highlight the significance of the stone above it.

Referring to the tablet above, the inscription on this stone reads:

This stone used for the ALTHAM memorial tablet was
preserved from the original tombstone of
THOMAS LORD
the founder of this ground, whose name is engraved on
its reverse side. He was buried at West Meon, Hampshire in
1832 and his grave was restored in 1951
by
M.C.C.

19. Statue of Rupert Fehr

Inside the Museum, on the right-hand side of the ground floor, is a life-sized statue of a schoolboy holding a cricket bat.

The boy is Rupert James Fehr (1908–16), whose life was tragically cut short during the First World War. He became ill and died after contracting an illness from soldiers who had been billeted in the Fehr family home. The statue was created posthumously by his uncle, Henry Charles Fehr – a renowned sculptor – using photographs of Rupert. In 1971, the statue was presented to MCC by Rupert's sisters as a long-term loan. Henry Fehr's signature can be seen on the plinth at the rear.

Statue of Rupert Fehr created by Henry Fehr. (JL)

Henry Fehr was born in Forest Hill, London, in 1867 to Swiss parents. He was active during the late nineteenth and early twentieth centuries. He spent many of his formative years in East London, living in Leyton before moving to South Kensington. Fehr was known for producing sculptures and several notable war memorials throughout the 1920s, including the Cenotaph in Leeds, the Queen Victoria Memorial in Hull, the Welsh dragon atop Cardiff's City Hall, and the statues and bas-reliefs on the courthouse of Middlesex Guildhall on Parliament Square, Westminster – now the building that houses the Supreme Court. Fehr's best-known work, *Perseus Rescuing Andromeda* (1893), is located outside on the right-hand balcony of Tate Britain in London. Henry Charles Fehr died in London on 13 May 1940.

20. Bust of Harold ('Dickie') Bird

The twentieth subject in this collection is located just inside the Museum's entrance. There are three busts, one of which depicts Harold Dennis 'Dickie' Bird, OBE. Born on 19 April 1933, Bird is a former professional cricketer who represented Yorkshire and Leicestershire. He is better known as a retired international cricket umpire, admired for his excellence in that role and for some eccentricities. The bust was created by Neale Andrew, the son of former Northamptonshire and England wicketkeeper Keith Andrew.

Born in Barnsley, Yorkshire, the son of a coal miner, Bird left school at fifteen and began working in a coal mine. However, he soon left that job to pursue a career in sports, initially in football and eventually in cricket. He signed with Yorkshire in 1956 and later joined Leicestershire in 1960. During his eight-year career, Bird scored only two centuries and was later omitted from the team due to a combination of injury, loss of form, and lack of confidence. His playing career ended at the age of thirty-one because of a knee injury.

'Dickie' Bird bust by Neale Andrew. (JL)

Bird became an umpire and officiated at his first county game in 1970. In 1973, he umpired his first Test match – England v New Zealand at Headingley, Leeds. This was the third and final Test of the series, which England won convincingly. That summer, he also umpired two Tests in the England v West Indies series. In the Edgbaston Test, Bird had to umpire from both ends for a few overs, with a substitute official standing at square leg. Bird's colleague Arthur Fagg refused to stand in protest against the behaviour of some West Indian players. In the next Test at Lord's, an Irish Republican Army (IRA) bomb threat led to the ground being evacuated. Bird chose not to leave the field of play, opting to sit on the outfield with the players until the false alarm was resolved.

Bird officiated in sixty-six Test matches and sixty-nine One Day Internationals, including three World Cup Finals at Lord's in 1975, 1979, and 1983. During the Centenary Test between England and Australia at Lord's in 1980, Bird and his fellow umpire David Constant delayed play due to overnight rain, despite the sunshine that day. This caused frustration among some MCC Members, who audibly and physically expressed their anger. The captains – Ian Botham of England and Greg Chappell of Australia – intervened to protect Constant, while Bird remained on the pitch. Play eventually resumed, and police escorted Bird and Constant through the Long Room and onto the field of play.

Despite these and many other similar incidents, Bird's eccentricities, good humour, and ability as an umpire endeared him to both players and spectators. At the start of his last Test match in 1996, the England and India players formed a guard of honour for him. A tearful Bird also received a standing ovation from the crowd. However, reality soon returned when, during the first over, he had to give Michael Atherton out lbw. Bird continued to umpire in county cricket for another two years, retiring in 1998.

Bird received an MBE (Member of the Order of the British Empire) in 1986 and an OBE (Officer of the Order of the British Empire) in 2012. A statue of Bird was unveiled in Barnsley in June 2009. Harold Bird died in September 2025, aged ninety-two.

21. Bust of Sir George Allen

The second bust close to the Museum's entrance is of Sir George Oswald Browning Allen, CBE. An important figure in the history of Lord's, Allen was born in Australia on 31 July 1902 and died on 29 November 1989. George Allen was better known as 'Gubby' – a nickname from his days at Eton, where his initials (G. O. B.) were used to create 'Gobby', and ultimately, 'Gubby'. Like the bust of Harold Bird, this one is also the work of Neale Andrew and was presented to MCC in 1986 by De Zoete Bevan.

During his first-class career, Allen represented both Middlesex and Cambridge University, captaining England in eleven Test matches. As a fast bowler and powerful lower-order batsman, he was a dominant figure during his playing days and later became an influential cricket administrator. He held key positions within the hierarchy of MCC and also served as Chairman of the England selectors.

Early Life

Allen was privately educated before attending Eton College and Cambridge University. He played cricket for the university in 1922 and received his Blue after selection for

Bust of Sir George Allen. (JL)

the University Match against Oxford at Lord's. In the following season, Allen played a few games for Middlesex CCC and was later chosen to represent the Gentlemen against the Players at Scarborough. After early successes with Middlesex in 1926, Allen was considered for possible selection for England against Australia that summer. However, he was unsuccessful on this occasion, as the selectors opted for Harold Larwood.

A combination of injuries and work commitments limited the amount of cricket that Allen could play in the following few years. However, he performed well against Lancashire in 1929, taking 10-40 in the first innings and becoming only the second man, after Alfred Shaw in 1874, to take all ten wickets in a first-class innings at Lord's. Despite this achievement, he was once again overlooked by the England selectors for the South Africa series.

Test Selection

In 1930, Allen was once again in contention for an England Test place in the series against Australia. Early-season successes led to his debut in the Test side for the match at Lord's. This selection was criticised by the press, who viewed Allen as injury-prone and inconsistent, as well as being Australian-born. England scored 425 in the first innings, and in response – with Allen opening the bowling – the Australian openers scored 162 before losing their first wicket. Don Bradman* eventually scored 254 runs, and Australia closed on 729-6 declared. Allen's return was 0-115 from thirty-four overs, and England lost the match. This was Allen's only Test match in this series.

*Don Bradman

Don Bradman in 1930. (MCC)

England was the favourite to win the Ashes in the 1930 series held in England. The Australians were pinning their hopes on several young batsmen, particularly the twenty-one-year-old Don Bradman. Bradman started strongly with 236 runs against Worcestershire and completed 1,000 first-class runs before the end of May. During that Test series, Bradman scored a total of 974 runs, including scores of 131, 254, 334 (a world record at the time), and 232. He averaged 139.14 in the series. Undoubtedly, Bradman's performances in this series laid the groundwork for the 'Bodyline' controversy that would arise a year or two later.

Bradman's Test career ended in 1948 when, in the fifth Test of the Ashes series at the Oval, he was bowled second ball for a duck by Eric Hollies. In fifty-two Test matches (80 innings), with twenty-nine centuries, Bradman had scored 7,996 runs. He needed just four runs in that last innings to average 100 in Test cricket, finishing his Test career with an impressive average of 99.94.

Despite playing little cricket in 1931, Allen was included in the England team for the Lord's Test match against New Zealand after Larwood's withdrawal. This selection was made by Pelham Warner, reportedly without consulting his fellow selectors, who were displeased with the decision. Allen scored 122 in England's first innings, his only innings in the series. He played in the other two Test matches that year and ended the series with eight wickets, averaging 16.12 each.

Allen did not feature in the only Test match in 1932 – India's first-ever Test match. However, he performed well in the Gentlemen v Players match, taking eight wickets. As a result of that performance, he was named in MCC's touring team to Australia for the upcoming winter. Once again, the press was critical of this selection due to Allen's first-class batting and bowling averages. Having been named in the tour party, he did not play any more cricket that season.

Bodyline

MCC's tour of Australia in 1932–33 was controversial due to the England team's use of what came to be known as 'Bodyline' bowling – an intimidatory tactic essentially instigated by MCC's captain, Douglas Jardine, to limit Don Bradman's prolific scoring.

In his book *The Book of Cricket*, Pelham Warner, the manager of MCC's team in Australia in 1932/33, contended that:

> Body-line bowling was first seen in England about 1910, when W. B. Burns, who for a few overs was terribly fast, bowled it for Worcestershire v. Middlesex, at Lord's. He, like Larwood, places seven men on the leg-side – six of them in the short-leg area; but this form of attack met with instant disapproval and was not persisted with.

Warner stated that he had objected then, and that his view never wavered.

In the first Test of the series, Allen unsettled and ultimately dismissed Bradman with his pace. He played in all five Tests and performed exceptionally well. Despite frequent requests from Jardine, he refused to employ the Bodyline tactics demanded by the captain, which made him popular with the Australian crowds. However, Jardine's other fast bowlers – Harold Larwood and Bill Voce – adhered to the strategy. Despite his opposition to Bodyline, Allen fielded in the so-called 'leg trap' and took five catches off Larwood's bowling during the series.

Captaincy

In 1936, Allen was named as England captain for the home series against India, replacing Bob Wyatt. He also captained the MCC team in the subsequent series in Australia, with Pelham Warner playing a key role in his appointment. Additional factors likely included his Australian origins and the need to heal rifts from the Bodyline series.

Allen was in the running to become England captain for the 1938 Ashes series, but Walter Hammond, a former professional who had turned amateur, was ultimately chosen. This decision irritated Allen, particularly since Warner had not consulted him about it.

Second World War and Retirement

In 1938, Allen was commissioned into the Territorial Army. He held several posts during the war before becoming a flak liaison officer for an RAF Bomber Command group. During this time, Allen became friends with Arthur 'Bomber' Harris. Allen eventually achieved the rank of Lieutenant Colonel.

After the war, Allen played little cricket. He was asked to captain and manage an MCC team that toured the West Indies. His age at the time and some personality clashes created an unpleasant atmosphere within the tour group. Allen made his final first-class appearance for the Free Foresters in 1954. During his career, he scored over 9,000 runs and took 788 wickets.

Cricket Administration

His playing career over, Allen focused on the game's administration and became a strong influence on the welfare of players and the development of cricket. He helped prominent retired professional cricketers to secure honorary MCC memberships and became involved in MCC's drive to improve youth cricket, especially in state schools. In 1951, he contributed to the compilation of *The MCC Cricket Coaching Book*.

As Chairman of the England selectors between 1955 and 1961, he promoted the causes of younger amateur batsmen, including Ted Dexter and Colin Cowdrey. Some professional cricketers believed that Allen was a snob who preferred to keep the professional players in their place. During the 1956 Ashes series, Allen was criticised in the press after making Fred Trueman bowl at a handkerchief before a match in an attempt to improve his accuracy. A large crowd witnessed this and, reportedly, Trueman felt humiliated. In 1963, MCC abolished the distinction between amateurs and professionals, a change that Allen opposed. That same year, Allen became MCC President and later served a twelve-year tenure as Treasurer.

Final Years

Allen left the MCC Treasurer's role in 1976. He became a CBE in 1962 and was knighted in 1986. Since 1968, Allen had lived in a house directly behind the Lord's Pavilion and remained there until his death. He spent a great deal of time in MCC's Committee Room, watching cricket. He died on 29 November 1989 and is buried at Brookwood Cemetery in Brookwood, Surrey. In 2023, MCC funded the restoration of Allen's grave.

22. Bust of Lord Harris

The third bust in the Museum's entrance area portrays George Robert Canning Harris (better known as Lord Harris). The artist remains unknown, and it is believed that the piece was created at the end of the nineteenth century. More information about Lord Harris's life and career can be found in an earlier section (see Number 8 – Harris Memorial Tablet).

Bust of Lord Harris. (JL)

23. Museum Window

This stained-glass window is located to the right of the MCC Museum entrance. It was unveiled by then Prime Minister John Major on 19 May 1993 to commemorate the restoration of the Museum. Designed by Philippa Mary Martin, her initials are visible in the bottom right corner. It depicts a view of the Ground from the Pavilion End, showing the Nursery End and the early versions of both the Compton and Edrich stands. The distinctive canopies of the 1987 Mound Stand are visible to the right.

Above: Window to commemorate the Museum's 1993 refurbishment.

Right: Detail of the window's dedication. (JL)

24. Lord's Sparrow

This item is related to a specific event that occurred at Lord's on 2 July 1936. An MCC team was playing Cambridge University when Jehangir Khan, a law student at Cambridge, bowled to T. N. (Tom) Pearce of MCC. The game was meandering towards a draw when one of Khan's deliveries prompted Pearce to play forward. Although he struck the ball with his bat, something hit the stumps behind him. As the players gathered around, they discovered a dead sparrow next to the stumps. According to reports, Khan's delivery had struck the sparrow, which was flying across the pitch, killing it instantly. A later account in *Wisden* noted that 'T. N. Pearce, the batsman, managed to play the ball and the bird fell against the stumps without dislodging a bail.'

After the match, the bird was treated with due respect and given to one of London's leading taxidermists, whose identity has been lost to history. It was mounted on the ball that killed it and was subsequently displayed in the Memorial Gallery (now the Museum) at Lord's.

The sparrow is displayed as if in flight, mounted on a cricket ball placed on a plinth. The inscription on the plinth reads:

THIS SPARROW WAS KILLED AT LORD'S BY A BALL
BOWLED BY JEHANGIR KHAN (CAMBRIDGE UNIVERSITY)
TO T. N. PEARCE (MCC)
ON JULY 3RD 1936

The sparrow has been a prominent fixture at MCC's Museum for many years and, as Neil Robinson (Head of Heritage & Collections at MCC) has said, 'Those who don't know

The Lord's Sparrow. (MCC)

the story are always surprised. The unexpected presence of the sparrow, as well as its sensational story, makes it a unique object in the museum's collection. The sparrow helps people to appreciate that even a cricket museum can be full of unusual objects.'

Over the years, the sparrow has become increasingly fragile. In 2020, it received care and attention at the Natural History Museum in Kensington. The conservation work included wire repairs and dry cleaning. It was also noted that the sparrow had severe skin splits and a loose wing. Damage from exposure to light was a concern, along with the accumulation of dust and grime over many decades.

25. Statuette of C. B. Fry

In a cabinet in the Museum there is a statuette of Charles Burgess (C. B.) Fry in cricketing action. It was created by the sculptor Albert Bruce-Joy around 1905. The statuette has previously been displayed in the Long Room and the Committee Dining Room. It is possible that MCC acquired it shortly after its creation.

Statuette of C. B. Fry. (MCC)

Fry was born in Croydon on 25 April 1872. He was educated at Repton School and Wadham College, Oxford, where he achieved a first-class honours degree in classical moderations. Not only was Fry a brilliant scholar, but at both Repton and Oxford there were signs that he had the potential to develop into an all-round athlete. Indeed, at Oxford, Fry gained twelve sporting 'Blues', excelling in cricket, rugby, athletics, boxing, golf, swimming, tennis, rowing, and javelin.

He was also an accomplished footballer, initially playing as an amateur for The Corinthians before becoming a professional with Southampton. In December 1900, he made his debut for Southampton against Tottenham Hotspur, and a few months later, he was chosen to represent England against Ireland. Fry played for Southampton in the final of the 1901/02 FA Cup against Sheffield United at Crystal Palace in front of a crowd of nearly 75,000. The match ended in a draw, but Southampton lost the replay.

Fry excelled as a track and field athlete, equalling the world long jump record in 1893 with a leap of 23 feet, 6 and a half inches. The following year, the world's first international athletics event took place at London's White City Stadium, where Fry emerged victorious in both the long jump and the 100-yard sprint events.

However, Fry's most notable sporting successes were on the cricket field, where he served as captain of both Sussex and England. Indeed, England never lost a Test match with Fry as captain. He scored more than 30,000 first-class runs, averaging just over fifty, which included ninety-four centuries.

Fry led an interesting life outside cricket, standing for Parliament in Brighton as a Liberal, serving as a director of a training ship, and working as a journalist. At the instigation of his former Sussex teammate Ranjitsinhji, he travelled to the newly created League of Nations in Geneva, established after the First World War. Fry's role was to write speeches for Indian representatives. While there, Fry claimed to have been offered the vacant Albanian throne. Apparently, the Albanian delegation at the League of Nations sought an English gentleman with an annual income of £10,000 to take their throne. While he was well qualified regarding the first condition, Fry did not meet the second one.

At the age of forty-nine, Fry attempted a cricket comeback and performed well against the touring Australians. Indeed, he was later offered the England captaincy. However, he declined the offer and retired from cricket soon after.

In 1898, Fry married Beatrice Sumner, who was ten years his senior. The couple had three children, but all was not well in the marriage. Beatrice was known for her aggressive personality and for being cruel and domineering toward her family. By all accounts, Fry lived in fear of her and distanced himself from her as much as possible. Fry experienced mental health issues and suffered a breakdown. Following Beatrice's death after forty-eight years of marriage, Fry and their children felt a sense of relief. Their son Stephen said later, 'my mother ruined my father's life'.

C. B. Fry died in 1956, in Hampstead, London, at the age of eighty-four.

THE STANDS

Exiting the Museum and heading north from the Pavilion, all the stands have been built, developed, and subsequently replaced numerous times since Thomas Lord brought MCC to this Ground in 1814. On a clockwise circumnavigation of the Ground, the first stand encountered is the Warner Stand, followed by the Grand Stand, then the Compton, Edrich, Mound, Tavern, and Allen Stands.

26. Warner Stand

Until 1958, the area now occupied by the Warner Stand was known as Block 'A', and dated from the early years of the twentieth century. In fact, all the seating areas at Lord's were initially designated by letters, beginning with Block 'A' and ending with the stand next to the Pavilion, which was Block 'Q' – now known as the Allen Stand.

Block 'A' was located at the north end of the Pavilion. In the nineteenth century, it consisted of little more than a few rows of covered seating. Behind these seats was the coach mound – a raised area of grass lined with trees from which spectators could watch the Ground's more established games from the comfort of their carriages. Due to the increasing number of MCC Members and the desire to reduce the thirty-year waiting list for membership at that time, there was a need to redevelop this area.

In 1958, the new stand was completed and incorporated a press box with space for 105 cricket journalists. MCC broke with tradition when deciding what to call the new stand. The Committee chose to honour a man whose career in cricket and association with Lord's Cricket Ground spanned nearly seventy years. Sir Pelham 'Plum' Warner* had been a player, captain, manager, and administrator since before the turn of the century. He captained MCC's first overseas tour – to Australia in 1903–04. His playing career lasted twenty-six years and included fifteen Test matches for England. He also captained Middlesex when they won the County Championship in 1920, Warner's final season. He managed Douglas Jardine's England team on the infamous 'Bodyline' tour to Australia in 1932–33. Warner was an MCC Committee Member, Deputy Secretary, Trustee, Club's President and, in 1961, he became the Club's first Life Vice-President.

Sir Pelham Warner officially opened the new Warner Stand, designed by Kenneth Peacock and constructed at a cost of £100,000, in 1958. The press box was located on the upper level of the Warner Stand, at its rear. In addition to this dedicated area, the press and broadcast media utilised the Pavilion's turrets. There was considerable dissatisfaction with this arrangement, as the press area was viewed as cold, draughty, and cramped, with a poor view. These issues ultimately led to the construction of the Media Centre in 1999 (see Number 33 – Media Centre).

*Sir Pelham Warner

Pelham Warner on a 1912 Murray's cigarettes card. (MCC)

Born in Trinidad on 2 October 1873, Sir Pelham Francis Warner, MBE, was an England Test cricketer and a renowned cricket administrator. He was known throughout the cricketing world as 'Plum'. Educated initially in Barbados, he was then sent to England, where he attended Rugby School, followed by Oriel College, Oxford. He played first-class cricket for Oxford University, Middlesex, and England.

A right-handed batsman, Warner played in just fifteen Test matches and captained his country in ten of them, winning four and losing six. Three of those victories occurred in the 1903–04 Ashes series in Australia. He was selected as captain for the 1911–12 tour to Australia, but had to withdraw from the team due to illness that struck after the opening match in Adelaide.

In 1904 and again in 1921, Warner was named the *Wisden* Cricketer of the Year. Only Jack Hobbs has also received the honour twice. The second occasion coincided with Warner's retirement as a Middlesex cricketer after leading them to the County Championship title in 1920. His final first-class match was for MCC against the Royal Navy in 1929.

Warner turned to cricket administration, becoming Chairman of the England Selectors. He was also England's Tour Manager, most notably during the 'Bodyline' tour to Australia in 1932–33. In the 1937 Coronation Honours list, he was knighted for services to cricket and became MCC President in 1950.

Warner founded *The Cricketer* magazine in 1921 and wrote a history of Lord's Cricket Ground, along with detailing his experiences in Ashes cricket. From 1921 to 1933, he served as the cricket correspondent for the *Morning Post* and later for the *Daily Telegraph*.

The 'Grand Old Man of Cricket', Pelham Warner, died aged eighty-nine on 30 January 1963 in West Lavington, West Sussex.

In 2012, MCC commissioned a master plan for Lord's from the architecture firm Populus. Its eventual aim was to replace five stands – Warner, Compton, Edrich, Tavern, and Allen – and to improve the Ground's facilities. The first stand to be addressed under this plan was the Warner Stand.

At a cost of £21 million, the new Warner Stand provides spectators with significantly improved sightlines and enhanced accessibility. Furthermore, the facilities for match officials and security personnel have been upgraded. Robert Ebdon, MCC's Assistant Secretary, said of the Warner Stand: 'MCC has always sought to commission innovative, unique buildings and stands that add to and complement the heritage of the ground and its surroundings. Populous' design does just that, and this truly outstanding facility will be enjoyed by visitors to Lord's for many years to come.'

The Duke of Edinburgh officially opened the Warner Stand on 3 May 2017. This was one of his last public engagements, and upon performing the ceremony, he said that 'you are about to see the world's most experienced plaque unveiler'.

The inscription on the plaque is difficult to read and is reproduced here:

THE ORIGINAL WARNER STAND OPENED BY
HIS GRACE THE DUKE OF NORFOLK, K.C., G.C.V.O.
AND SIR PELHAM WARNER
OCCUPIED THIS SITE BETWEEN 1958 AND 2015

THIS WARNER STAND WAS OPENED BY
HIS ROYAL HIGHNESS THE PRINCE PHILIP, DUKE OF EDINBURGH, K.G., K.T.
PRESIDENT OF M.C.C. 1949 AND 1975
ON 3RD MAY 2017

The opening of the second Warner Stand in 2017. (JL)

The Warner Stand in 2025. (JL)

27. Grand Stand

Another plaque unveiled by The Duke of Edinburgh is located at the rear of the current Grand Stand. The stand was opened on 18 June 1998, and the plaque commemorates the construction of the third stand on this site.

The first Grand Stand was opened in 1867, funded by a private syndicate of MCC Members. *The Illustrated London News* of 10 August 1867 reported that 'a limited company was formed, consisting of fifteen members of the club, to provide the means for carrying out this scheme'. The entire project was completed within three months. The new stand measured 200 feet in length and could accommodate 600 spectators. This first Grand Stand included a private box for the exclusive use of the Prince of Wales, as well as space for a printing office, and provided members of the press with their first dedicated area. Marylebone Cricket Club purchased the stand from the Members' syndicate in 1869.

In the 1920s, MCC planned to redevelop the Grand Stand and enlisted the help of a trusted architect, Sir Herbert Baker, who was responsible for designing the Grace Gates. The project to rebuild the Grand Stand faced delays due to several factors, including the General Strike in 1926. Upon completion, a weathervane representing Father Time was placed atop Baker's Grand Stand and remained there until the stand was replaced with the current structure. It was then relocated to its new home above the clock tower, directly opposite the current Grand Stand (see Number 37 – Father Time Weathervane). The weathervane has long been understood to have been a gift from Baker to MCC as an apology for the late completion of the stand. However, no written evidence has been found in MCC's archive to confirm this.

Commemorating Lord's third Grand Stand opened in 1998. (JL)

Although Baker's Grand Stand soon became a well-known and recognisable feature at Lord's Ground, it was not an ideal place to watch cricket, as a significant percentage of the seats had restricted views. By the 1990s, much of the structure had deteriorated.

With Lord's Ground scheduled to host matches in the 1999 International Cricket Council (ICC) Cricket World Cup – including the final – it became evident that the Grand Stand urgently needed upgrading. The architect appointed was Nicholas Grimshaw, who completed the project in stages. The lower terrace, comprising 4,200 seats, was finished on schedule and was in use for the 1997 season. The following winter, the remainder of the stand was completed, and the new structure was officially opened by The Duke of Edinburgh on 18 June 1998. In *The Times*, Michael Henderson wrote, 'even the mizzle of a grey London morning could not deny the splendour of the new stand'.

Lord's Grand Stand in 2023. (JL)

MCC was delighted with the new Grand Stand, not only for its appearance but also because the project was completed within budget and in time for the start of the England v South Africa Test match in mid-June 1998.

28. Compton Stand

Denis Charles Scott Compton, CBE, was born on 23 May 1918 in the Hendon area of north London. Along with Bill Edrich (see Number 29 – Edrich Stand), he was part of the renowned 'Middlesex Twins', who dominated county cricket in general, and cricket at Lord's in particular, for many years.

Compton was one of the best-known athletes of his era, with a reputation as one of England's most accomplished and talented batsmen. This ability, combined with his charisma, made him a national idol. He enjoyed a glittering career, scoring over 100 first-class centuries (123 in total) – the thirteenth player to achieve that milestone. He spent his entire cricket career at Middlesex and represented England in Test cricket on seventy-eight occasions. He was also an accomplished footballer, making fifty-four appearances for Arsenal as a winger. Compton additionally represented England in twelve wartime football matches, although these were not official internationals. Notably, he is the only person to have won the county cricket championship and the FA Cup in the same year – 1950.

Compton was a right-handed batsman and a slow left-arm wrist-spin bowler. At just over nineteen years of age, he made his Test debut during England's series against New Zealand in 1937. Just a year later, he scored his maiden Test century against Bradman's Australian touring side. This broke J. W. Hearne's record – set in 1911 – for being the youngest English Test centurion. In the 1939 season, Compton scored 2,468 runs, including another Test century against the West Indies at Lord's.

In common with many prominent athletes of the 1930s, Compton lost a significant portion of his career due to the Second World War, during which he served in the Army in India. It was there that he met Keith Miller – an Australian Test cricketer and national hero. The two became firm friends for the rest of their lives, and in recognition of this and their lasting influence on cricket, the ECB and Cricket Australia decided in 2005 that from then on, the Player of the Series in the Ashes contests would be awarded the Compton–Miller medal.

Compton's reputation was that of a playboy, and there are stories of him arriving for a cricket match at Lord's still dressed in the previous evening's dinner suit. His personality, looks, and reputation led to his image being used to advertise a hair treatment product – Compton was 'The Brylcreem Boy'.

He also had a reputation for inconsistently calling to his batting partner. His England colleague Trevor Bailey once famously said, 'A call from Denis was merely the basis for negotiation.' At a 1955 benefit match for his brother, Leslie, Denis managed to run him out before he had faced a single ball.

Due to persistent knee problems, Compton retired prematurely, having illuminated the cricket world both before and after the Second World War. He scored nearly 39,000 first-class runs, including 123 centuries. Denis Compton died in 1997 at the age of seventy-eight.

From 1924 until 1991, the stands at the Nursery End at Lord's – on either side of where the Media Centre is now situated – were known simply as 'G' and 'H' stands. These stands were designed by Sir Herbert Baker, who was also responsible for the 1926 Grand Stand and the 1923 Grace Gates. 'G' and 'H' were notorious for their poor sightlines from the lower decks, which offered just over 6 feet of headroom. This meant that watching cricket there was not unlike looking through a letterbox. In fact, Baker himself observed that 'the back row had a view of the game as far as the bottom of the Pavilion rails'. Any ball that was hit above head height would not have been visible from the lower decks of 'G' and 'H'.

When 'G' and 'H' stands were redeveloped by the architect Michael Hopkins, MCC decided to honour Denis Compton and Bill Edrich by naming the new stands after them. The first Compton and Edrich Stands at Lord's were opened in 1991 by Denis Compton himself. However, similar sighting problems affected the new stands. Additionally, there was a difference in temperature. It was said that if you sat on the upper tier, you ran the risk of sunstroke, while if you were on the lower tier, the risk was hypothermia.

The present stands, opened in 2021 by MCC President Kumar Sangakkara, have dramatically enhanced comfort and the viewing experience. They also increased the Ground's capacity by 2,600, and it is fitting that the two stands are still named after the two great Middlesex and England batsmen whose careers were so closely associated with each other.

The opening of the second Compton Stand in 2021. (JL)

29. Edrich Stand

William John Edrich, born on 26 March 1916 in Lingwood, Norfolk, was a first-class cricketer who played for Middlesex, MCC, England, and Norfolk. He came from a family steeped in cricket. His three brothers were all first-class cricketers, and his cousin was John Edrich, a distinguished opening batsman for Surrey and England for many years.

Edrich first played for Norfolk at the age of sixteen and became a Middlesex player in 1937. He made an immediate impact, scoring over 2,000 runs in that year. The following year, he scored 1,000 runs before the end of May and made his debut for England, with another thirty-eight appearances to follow. On the 1938–39 winter tour to South Africa, his 219 in the final 'Timeless Test' of the series helped England to 654-5. This was the longest Test match in history and was abandoned as a draw after nine days' play, spread over twelve days, as the England players had to catch their ship home.

When the Second World War started, Edrich joined the Royal Air Force, flying Bristol Blenheim bombers. He attained the rank of Squadron Leader and participated in the first-ever '1,000-bomber' raid. According to Denis Compton, one of Edrich's superstitions while flying was to wear his MCC sweater beneath his tunic. For his war service, Edrich was awarded the Distinguished Flying Cross (DFC). After the war, he expressed 'an immense relief that he survived'. This relief was reflected in the joy that both he and his batting partner, Compton, expressed in their cricketing careers after the war.

After the war, Edrich continued with the England side, batting at number three. During the hot summer of 1947, Edrich scored runs at an extraordinary rate, amassing a total of 3,539 runs, while Denis Compton accumulated 3,816 runs.

When his career ended in 1958, Edrich had played 571 first-class matches, scoring 36,985 runs with a top score of 267 not out. After retiring from Middlesex, Edrich rejoined Norfolk and continued to play Minor Counties cricket until he was fifty-six.

Edrich was married five times and had two sons. He died on 24 April 1986 at the age of seventy, following a fall at his home in Chesham, Buckinghamshire. Five years later, MCC

The opening of the second Edrich Stand in 2021. (JL)

The Compton and Edrich stands (2024) flanking the Media Centre. (JL)

named the stands at the Nursery End 'Edrich' and 'Compton' in his and Denis Compton's honour.

30. Mound and Tavern Stands

Mound Stand

The present Mound Stand is located on the site of the first Real Tennis Court, which was built in 1838. When that was demolished in the late 1890s and the Tennis Court was relocated to the area behind the Pavilion, the first Mound Stand was constructed in 1899 at a cost of £15,000. The new Mound Stand did not receive universal acclaim. On 15 July 1899, *The Graphic* reported:

> The huge new stand, oddly christened by the authorities 'the Mound', may have several advantages from the point of view of convenience, but it has nothing like the picturesqueness of the old arrangement and had dealt a death blow to the promenade.

Despite these initial reservations, the Mound Stand became a popular place from which to watch cricket. However, it needed to be redeveloped in the 1980s, as MCC aimed to celebrate its bicentenary in 1987 with an ambitious building project.

The design selected was submitted by Michael Hopkins & Partners, who skilfully combined the preservation of the original seven Victorian brick arches, constructed by Frank Verity, at the rear of the stand with a brand-new structure above. However, the project faced financial challenges due to a tight two-year deadline.

The project to improve the Mound Stand was partially funded by a generous donation from John Paul Getty II*. Introduced to the mysteries of cricket by his friend Mick Jagger from the Rolling Stones, Getty offered to pay 50 per cent of the original £3 million estimate. However, when costs rose by 45 per cent, Getty was prepared to cover the increased sum.

The completed Mound Stand received a warm reception from both MCC and spectators. The distinctive canopies, designed to resemble the marquees typically found at village, club, and festival cricket venues, were an immediate success. The stand was officially opened by The Duke of Edinburgh on 6 May 1987.

*John Paul Getty II

Born on 7 September 1932, on a ship near Genoa, Italy, Sir Paul Getty KBE, better known as John Paul Getty Jr, was the son of J. Paul Getty, one of the world's wealthiest men. The Getty family's wealth originated from the oil industry.

After his father died in 1976, Getty suffered from depression. He spent significant time at The London Clinic in Devonshire Place, London, where he met Mick Jagger. Later, Getty purchased Wormsley Park in Buckinghamshire, where he established a cricket ground. The opening match in 1992 was attended by notable guests, including Queen Elizabeth, the Queen Mother, and Prime Minister John Major.

In addition to donating money to support the development of the Mound Stand at Lord's, Getty also contributed significant amounts to various causes, including the Imperial War Museum and the British Film Institute. In 1986, he received an honorary knighthood for his charitable work. He became a British citizen in 1997, which permitted him to use the title granted to him earlier.

John Paul Getty II died at The London Clinic in April 2003 at the age of seventy, following a chest infection.

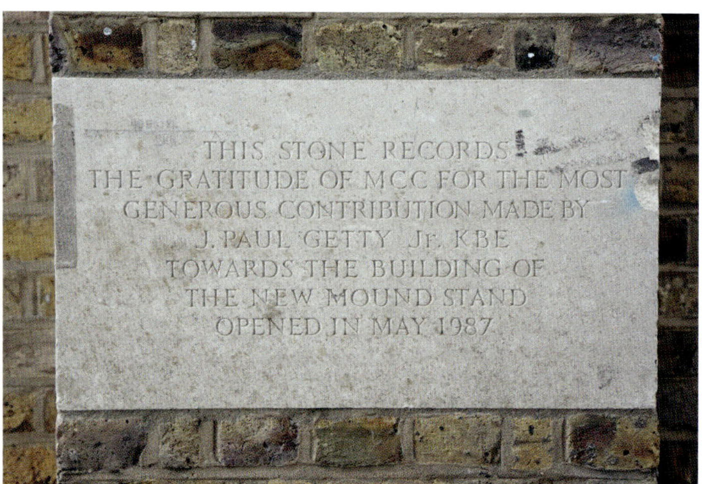

Getty's contribution to the redevelopment of the Mound Stand is remembered. (JL)

The Mound Stand in 2025. (JL)

The weathered inscription on the stone reads:

THIS STONE RECORDS
THE GRATITUDE OF MCC FOR THE MOST
GENEROUS CONTRIBUTION MADE BY
J. PAUL GETTY Jr. KBE
TOWARDS THE BUILDING OF
THE NEW MOUND STAND
OPENED IN MAY 1987

Tavern Stand

Located between the Mound and Allen stands is the Tavern Stand. When Thomas Lord established MCC at its current location in 1814, he added two significant new facilities at the Ground – a Pavilion for the players and Members, and a pub for the patrons. Lord's first public house stood on the site until 1867, and its successor lasted a further ninety-nine years, known as Lord's Hotel, but better known as the Tavern. The development was funded by an advance of £4,000 from the gin magnate William Nicholson. A few years earlier, Nicholson had helped MCC to buy the freehold of Lord's.

The Tavern's bars and dining rooms were always well attended during major matches, with the catering business managed by the redoubtable George Portman, who ran it between 1902 and 1950. Under Portman's direction, the Lord's Tavern prepared and served approximately 3,000 lunches and 6,000 teas on each major match day. Portman also operated a bakery and confectionery that sold homemade ice cream, chocolates, and other sweets. This was so popular that queues formed along St John's Wood Road.

The Tavern Stand in 2025. (JL)

The Tavern was a much-loved institution and a very sociable place to watch cricket, especially for the Lord's Taverners. The Taverners is a sporting charity founded in 1950 by several BBC personalities and actors, including Brian Johnston, John Snagge, John Mills, and Jack Hawkins. The idea stemmed from their interest in watching cricket from Lord's Tavern, one of the few venues in London with a licence to serve alcohol in the afternoon.

However, during the 1960s, it became clear that the old Tavern was no longer fit for purpose and could not support a modern catering business. The Tavern was demolished in 1966 and replaced by the current stand designed by Kenneth Peacock. A new Tavern pub was built next to the Grace Gates.

31. Allen Stand

The Allen Stand is located between the Tavern Stand and the Pavilion. The redevelopment of the stand in the 1930s aligned with the Committee's objective of increasing MCC membership from 6,000 to approximately 7,000. The design of the stand included a walkway leading into the Pavilion.

Designed by Sir Herbert Baker and opened as 'Q' Block in the mid-1930s, the stand was refurbished and renamed in 1989 as a tribute to the Middlesex and England cricketer Sir George 'Gubby' Allen (1902–89). Along with the Tavern Stand, the Allen Stand is scheduled for redevelopment in the next year or so (see Number 21 for more on the life of Gubby Allen).

Neale Andrew's bust of Sir George Allen in the Allen Stand. (JL)

The inscription below the bust of Allen reads:

SIR GEORGE
ALLEN
CBE
IN WHOSE HONOUR
THIS
STAND WAS NAMED
BY THE MCC COMMITTEE
IN AUGUST 1989

The Allen Stand in 2023. (JL)

AROUND THE GROUND

32. Father Time Wall

Between the Grand Stand and the Compton Stand, on the north side of the Ground, a new installation has taken shape in recent years – the Father Time Wall. The wall consists of three sections.

Firstly, the larger images commemorate the two England One Day International fifty-over World Cup successes in recent years. On the left, the England women's victory over India in 2017 is celebrated, and on the right, the England men's defeat of New Zealand in 2019 is highlighted. In both images, the moment of victory is depicted as Heather Knight and Eoin Morgan lift the respective trophies.

Secondly, across the centre of the installation are 100 cream-coloured plaques. These illustrate the most significant milestones at Lord's Cricket Ground, and they were voted for by MCC Members. Listed below are the 'First XI' of the cream-coloured plaques:

1787: **No. 1.** – THOMAS LORD ESTABLISHES A CRICKET GROUND AT DORSET FIELDS
The birth of Marylebone Cricket Club

2019: **No. 2.** – ENGLAND BEATS NEW ZEALAND TO WIN THE MEN'S WORLD CUP
The first tied World Cup Final, finally won by England, with more boundaries struck

The Father Time Wall. (JL)

1788: **No. 3.** – MCC ISSUES A CODE OF LAWS FOR CRICKET
MCC continues to hold the guardianship of the Laws of Cricket to this day

2017: **No. 4.** – ENGLAND BEATS INDIA TO WIN THE WOMEN'S WORLD CUP
The eleventh Women's World Cup, and England's fourth title

1928: **No. 5.** – THE ASHES URN IS PRESENTED TO MCC
Created in 1882, the Ashes Urn stands as a powerful symbol of the England vs Australia cricket rivalry

1890: **No. 6.** – THOMAS VERITY'S NEW PAVILION IS COMPLETED
The third Pavilion on the site, built at a cost of £21,000, is the oldest building at Lord's

2017: **No. 7.** – ENGLAND'S JAMES ANDERSON TAKES HIS 500TH TEST WICKET
Anderson bowled out West Indian Kraigg Brathwaite to achieve this milestone

1990: **No. 8.** – GRAHAM GOOCH 333 – FIRST TEST TRIPLE-CENTURY AT LORD'S
The highest score achieved by any player in a Test match at Lord's

1922: **No. 9.** – MEMORIAL GATES ERECTED IN MEMORY OF W. G. GRACE
Following Grace's death in 1915, the Gates became a memorial to 'The Great Cricketer'

1975: **No. 10.** – WEST INDIES BEATS AUSTRALIA TO WIN THE FIRST MEN'S WORLD CUP
The first of three consecutive finals at Lord's contested for the Prudential World Cup

1926: **No. 11.** – THE FATHER TIME WEATHERVANE IS GIFTED TO MCC
Situated above the clock tower, it is one of the most recognisable symbols of Lord's

Lastly, the smaller blue plaques placed above and below the cream ones have been purchased by supporters and lovers of cricket. This initiative offered cricket supporters the chance to buy a personalised plaque, ensuring them a place on the Father Time Wall for a specific period. There are too many to describe here, but one pertains to a former Lord's Pavilion Steward, Ted Clark. After Ted died, his daughter arranged for a plaque for him that mentions the strict Pavilion dress code and reads, 'Not in those shoes, sir'.

The sale of plaques funded the project and provided a financial boost to the MCC Foundation (MCCF), an international cricket charity that delivers projects across the UK and around the world.

Remembering Ted Clark on The Father Time Wall. (JL)

33. Media Centre

During the 1990s, members of the press, along with radio and television commentators, became dissatisfied with the facilities available to them. The old press box, located at the rear of the first Warner Stand, was built in 1958. Additionally, the two turrets in the Pavilion were used to accommodate the broadcast media. Clearly, this was unsatisfactory, and a solution needed to be found as Lord's anticipated the arrival of the world's press for the 1999 Cricket World Cup.

MCC's Committee met in April 1995 and decided that a Media Centre should be constructed. The press lobbied for their new facilities to be positioned behind the bowler's arm, making the Nursery End of the Ground the only logical solution. However, this led to other practical difficulties. For example, if the Media Centre were constructed there, how would the ground staff be able to get their equipment onto the field of play? The gap between the Compton and Edrich stands was not large enough to accommodate a brand-new press area. The solution arrived at was a 'floating' Media Centre.

By the end of 1995, a design submitted by Future Systems had been chosen. Constructed in two shipyards – one in the Netherlands and the other in Cornwall – the structure was

The Lord's Media Centre. (JL)

The Media Centre on a busy match day. (JL)

completed in time for the 1999 World Cup and was officially opened on 27 April 1999 by MCC's President Tony Lewis along with a representative of the first sponsors, NatWest.

The Media Centre accommodates 144 journalists representing the written press on the lower level and features eight broadcast suites on the upper level. Scattered throughout the Media Centre are plaques commemorating distinguished Cricket Writers' Club members – Samuel Norman Bueno de Mesquita, John Woodcock, Reg Hayter, and Christopher Martin-Jenkins.

Samuel de Mesquita

Born on 28 January 1932, Samuel Norman Bueno de Mesquita was a respected journalist who specialised in cricket coverage. De Mesquita held various jobs, including working in

Plaque commemorating Samuel de Mesquita. (JL)

sales and advertising, before his passion for sport took over. His appetite for cricket was ignited when he attended a 1945 Lord's Victory Test. In 1970, he became the sports editor of BBC Radio London, and between 1973 and 2000, he wrote for *The Times* on cricket and other sports. He was a reassuring presence in the Media Centre, where he served as *Wisden*'s Middlesex correspondent. From 1945 onward, he attended at least one day of every Lord's Test match until he died at his home in London on 25 July 2013.

John Woodcock

John Woodcock was born on 7 August 1926 in the village of Longparish, Hampshire. He was educated at St. Edward's School in Oxford and Trinity College, Oxford, where he graduated with a degree in Geography. Later, he obtained a teaching qualification with the intention of pursuing that profession. However, his interest in cricket secured him a job at the BBC as a scorer during the Lord's Ashes Test in 1948.

Known as 'The Sage of Longparish', Woodcock initially wrote for *The Manchester Guardian* and, most notably, for *The Times*. He began with that newspaper in 1954 and served as its cricket correspondent until 1987, during which time he attended over 400 Test matches. He also wrote for and edited other publications, including the *Wisden Cricketers' Almanack* during the 1980s.

Woodcock served as President of the Cricket Writers' Club from 1986 to 2004 and received an OBE in 1996 for his contributions to sports journalism. After retiring, he served on MCC's Committee. Woodcock submitted his final article to *The Times* in July 2020 – a tribute to the West Indian cricketer Sir Everton Weekes. He passed away in July 2021 in Longparish at the age of ninety-four.

Plaque commemorating John Woodcock. (JL)

Plaque in honour of Reg Hayter. (JL)

Reg Hayter

Reginald Hayter, born on 4 December 1913 in Paddington, London, was a respected journalist and sports agency owner. After the Second World War, Hayter became the Press Association's chief cricket reporter, covering Test matches both at home and abroad. Sensing an opportunity to provide bespoke coverage to national and regional newspapers, Hayter launched his own sports news agency in February 1955. This venture included not only coverage of matches and events, but also feature writing and the publication of results and statistics. This approach was groundbreaking for its time. Hayter's deals with sports editors were based on trust, sealed with a firm handshake and recorded in a notebook.

He loved cricket and became friends with many of the game's greats over the years, serving as an adviser to Denis Compton, Ian Botham, Bill Edrich, Keith Miller, Godfrey Evans, and Basil D'Oliveira. He was also an adviser to notable figures in other sports, including Henry Cooper and Bob Wilson.

Hayter worked in Fleet Street for sixty years, and it is unlikely that many will match that longevity. His enthusiasm for life, for sportspeople, and for his fellow journalists was infectious. Reg Hayter died on 13 March 1994, at the age of eighty.

Christopher Martin-Jenkins

Christopher Dennis Alexander Martin-Jenkins, widely known as 'CMJ', was born on 20 January 1945 in Peterborough. He was a respected cricket writer and broadcaster, and also served as President of MCC. As the longest-serving commentator on BBC Radio's Test Match Special (TMS), his mellifluous tones and seemingly effortless style could be heard from 1973 until his cancer diagnosis in March 2012.

Martin-Jenkins attended St Bede's Preparatory School in Eastbourne before progressing to Marlborough College in Wiltshire. He became captain of the school cricket team and, around the same time, wrote to TMS's Brian Johnston asking for guidance on how he

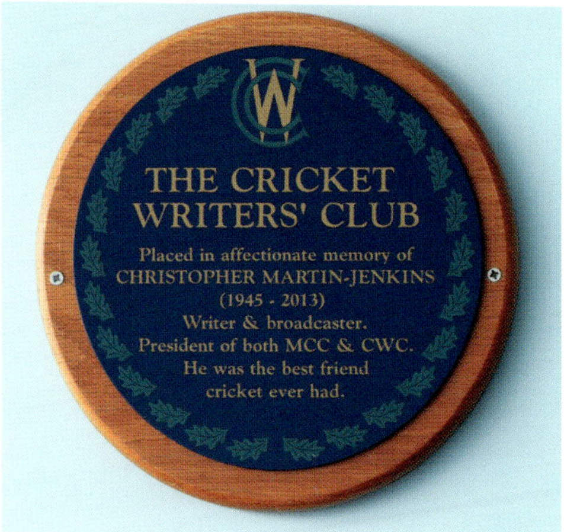

Christopher Martin-Jenkins is commemorated. (JL)

could become a cricket commentator. Johnston invited him to the BBC's Broadcasting House and offered him valuable advice.

He read Modern History at Cambridge and graduated in 1967. Shortly after, Martin-Jenkins joined *The Cricketer* magazine as deputy editor. He left three years later to join the BBC, where, in 1972, he commentated on his first match, a One Day International (ODI) between England and Australia.

He joined TMS the following year and became Brian Johnston's successor as the BBC's cricket correspondent in 1973. In addition to his many years with the BBC, Martin-Jenkins also wrote for *The Daily Telegraph* and *The Times* at various times. His final article concerned the death of former England captain Tony Greig and was published on 31 December 2012, the day before his own death.

He delivered his last radio commentary on England's third Test match against Pakistan in Dubai in February 2012. Scyld Berry wrote in *The Daily Telegraph*, 'What made him so good as a radio commentator, apart from his precise and unforced diction, was that he came closer than anyone to combining the knowledge of an expert with the enthusiasm of a student.'

Following his death in Horsham, Sussex, Christopher Martin-Jenkins's desk was donated to MCC and can be seen in MCC's Library.

34. MCC Indoor Cricket Centre

At the beginning of the twentieth century, MCC was receiving enquiries from Members who asked if they could bring their sons to Lord's during the Easter holidays to join them in the practice areas, and to occupy them while they were not at school. As a result, Easter Coaching Classes started in 1902. They were organised by MCC's Secretary at the time, Sir Francis Lacey, and the coaches were Lord's ground staff, whose regular duties included bowling to Members in the nets. Initially, there was no dedicated area on the Ground for this activity, so they utilised a covered area close to the Mound Stand.

However, the idea gained popularity, and by the early 1930s, Easter Coaching at Lord's attracted nearly 200 boys daily. Nets were set up on the Nursery Ground, but in case of rain, the coaches had to improvise by using the arbours – refreshment areas that surrounded the Nursery Ground.

Following the Second World War, MCC, encouraged by the 1949 MCC President, The Duke of Edinburgh, established a National Coaching Scheme. Its purpose was to oversee the training of cricket coaches and promote cricket coaching throughout the country.

There were several indoor cricket facilities in the London area, with the best-known being Alf Gover's Indoor School in Wandsworth. However, there was nothing of that kind at Lord's. In 1974, MCC proposed the construction of a covered school to be built at the Nursery End. Thanks to generous donations from various benefactors, including the Sports Council and Sir Jack Hayward, the Club's first Indoor School was inaugurated on 28 November 1977.

It was a success, and the Easter Coaching Classes were supplemented with additional sessions during the Christmas and summer holidays. The first indoor school closed in 1994 and was replaced by the current Indoor Cricket Centre, which was opened in 1995 by The Duke of Edinburgh.

The inscription on the plaque states:

M.C.C. Indoor School
was opened on
19th October 1995
by H.R.H. The Prince Philip,
Duke of Edinburgh, K.G., K.T.
President of M.C.C.
1949 and 1975

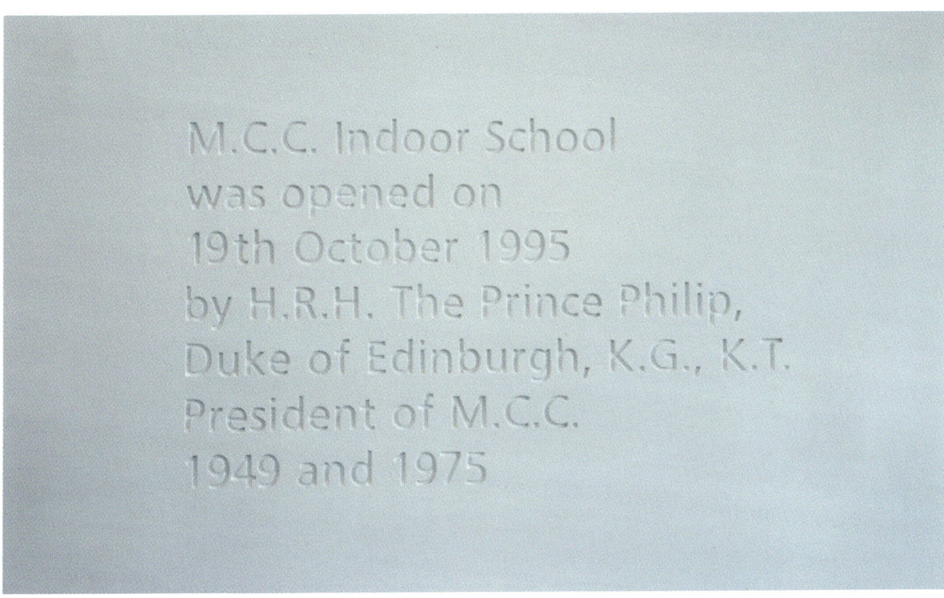

The opening of the Indoor Cricket Centre in 1995. (JL)

The Lord's Indoor Cricket Centre in 2022. (JL)

35. Batsman

Behind the Media Centre and facing the Nursery Ground are two statues. The first statue is called simply 'Batsman', and is also known as 'The Cover Drive'. Created by the sculptor Gerald Laing, this statue was cast, delivered, and installed by Black Isle Bronze in 2000. The 'Batsman' – like the 'Bowler' statue (see Number 36) – was originally positioned in Coronation Garden, where it was unveiled on 9 July 2001.

'Batsman' statue. (JL)

Gerald Ogilvie-Laing, born in Newcastle upon Tyne on 11 February 1936, was an artist and sculptor. He was educated at Berkhamsted School and then attended the Royal Military Academy, Sandhurst, before serving with the Royal Northumberland Fusiliers. However, realising that military life was not for him, he later enrolled at Saint Martin's School of Art in London.

In the early 1960s, during a trip to New York City, Laing met fellow artists Andy Warhol and Roy Lichtenstein. His career in art began to flourish when he later relocated to New York. He explored various genres, including pop art, minimalist sculpture, and representational sculpture. Several of his later works featured popular figures such as Victoria Beckham, Kate Moss, and Amy Winehouse. Laing died on 23 November 2011.

Inscribed on the plinth is:

MCC (logo)
BATSMAN
GERALD LAING 2001

36. Bowler

Behind the Media Centre, accompanying the 'Batsman', is a statue of a bowler. Called simply 'Bowler' but also known as 'Fast Bowler', it was created by Antony Dufort, a Council Member of the Society of Portrait Sculptors and a member of the Royal British Society of Sculptors.

'Bowler' statue. (Antony Dufort)

Antony Dufort kindly shared his experience of delivering the 'Bowler' statue to Lord's. He mentioned that in 2000, MCC's arts and library committee asked him and Gerald Laing to tender for sculptures of a bowler and a batsman for two corners of the Nursery Ground. Maquettes of the proposed designs were presented to the committee about six months later.

Dufort presented a figure of a fast bowler, substantially the same as the final statue. However, to convey a sense of dynamism and accurately position the muscles, his model – a dancer and keen amateur cricketer – posed wearing only a jockstrap. A discussion ensued about nudity in sculpture. Lord Fellowes, the committee Secretary and also Her Majesty the Queen's private Secretary, was asked for his opinion. Fellowes replied, 'If we want to be the laughing stock of the entire cricketing world, then a nude bowler would be a good idea.'

Following the meeting, Gerald Laing was awarded the commission for the batsman, while Antony Dufort received the commission for the bowler. It was hoped that a wicketkeeper and a fielder could be added to the other two corners of the Nursery Ground at a later date.

Antony Dufort admitted to me that he knew little about cricket. As part of his preparation for the model that was later presented, he obtained permission from MCC to film bowlers from a private box during a Test match. He then watched the footage in slow motion to analyse their bowling actions. He also reviewed archival film of famous fast bowlers. Ultimately, the aggressive style of Dennis Lillee served as an inspiration, but with a higher follow-through leg position.

The sculpture stands 9 feet tall from the base to the tip of its raised finger. It took over a year to create and an additional six months to cast. Made of bronze, which is only a quarter of an inch thick, it weighs more than 800 pounds. Inside the sculpture is a bent, solid stainless-steel rod (5 inches in diameter) that extends from above the knee, through the toe, and into the solid stone base.

Antony Dufort's expertise as a draftsman has significantly contributed to his proficiency in various artistic disciplines, including illustration, film storyboards, portrait painting, and public sculpture. In recent years, Dufort has sculpted the late Queen twice and produced a large sculpture of Margaret Thatcher for the Members' Lobby of the House of Commons. In case they are ever needed, Dufort has also created maquettes of a fielder and a wicketkeeper. His training as a historian has aided him in conducting the background research necessary to ensure that his subjects are depicted appropriately and realistically.

The former England captain Ted Dexter unveiled the 'Bowler' statue on 14 May 2002. Inscribed on the plinth is:

MCC (logo)
BOWLER
ANTONY DUFORT 2001

37. Father Time Weathervane

One of the most recognisable symbols of Lord's Ground is the Father Time Weathervane. The weathervane measures 6 feet 6 inches (1.98 metres), while the figure of Father Time itself stands at 5 feet 4 inches (1.63 metres). Father Time is a human representation of time, and this example depicts him either removing or replacing the bails on top of the stumps. On the opposite side of the stumps from Father Time is a ball, which may indicate that a wicket has just fallen. Additionally, on Father Time's back are a harvester's sickle and an hourglass shown as half full. These two symbols remind the onlooker that time moves unstoppably forward but, at the same time, offers renewal.

The weathervane is positioned above the clock tower, which is located between the Mound and Tavern stands and was initially placed on top of the 1926 Grand Stand. While there, it became the only casualty at Lord's during the Second World War when a steel cable from a barrage balloon became entangled and dragged it to the ground. Father Time spent the rest of the war in the Committee Room. It was eventually repaired and returned to its previous position. The weathervane was relocated to its current spot when Baker's Grand Stand was demolished in the 1990s.

In 1992, the weathervane was struck by lightning, and the subsequent repairs were featured on the BBC children's programme *Blue Peter*. In March 2015, Father Time was damaged once again, this time by high winds, which required extensive repairs by specialists.

The Father Time Weathervane. (JL)

THE PAVILION

The Pavilion at Lord's Cricket Ground. (JL)

38. Royal Charter

Upon entering the Pavilion, on the right side of the main rear entrance, is the impressive Royal Charter, which was granted to MCC on 12 December 2012.

It has always been challenging to define Marylebone Cricket Club in legal terms. Essentially, MCC is a private Members' Club, with the added responsibility of having a well-known public function. Due to this unclear legal status, MCC was unable to hold assets – including Lord's Ground – in its own name.

The first application for MCC to become a body incorporated by Royal Charter was made in 1864. This occurred during a period when the Ground was being developed, prior to Middlesex CCC becoming tenants, which limited the potential for income. The second attempt was in 1929 and was rejected on the grounds that a charter had never been granted to a sporting body, despite King George V being MCC's Patron at the time.

After nearly 150 years and three attempts, MCC's application was finally approved by Queen Elizabeth II during a Privy Council meeting on 12 December 2012. It took effect on 1 July 2013.

MCC's Royal Charter. (JL)

The Charter document was formally unveiled by HRH The Princess Anne, and its design features many familiar symbols associated with MCC, including the Ashes Urn and Father Time. Additionally, a pineapple is depicted as a tribute to Henderson's Nursery, which occupied the site of the Nursery Ground until MCC purchased the land to develop practice facilities in 1887.

39. MCC Presidents

On the ground floor of Verity's 1890 Pavilion, through two sets of double doors at the southern end of the Long Room, is the MCC Committee Room. Four boards with green backgrounds display the names of the Presidents of MCC from 1821 to the present day.

Records prior to 1821 were lost when a fire in the original wooden Pavilion on 28 July 1825 destroyed all documentation dating back to MCC's foundation in 1787. This incident is noted on the current Presidents' Board and was reported in the *Oxford Journal* on 6 August 1825 as follows:

> About one o'clock on Friday morning, a fire of a terrific nature broke out in the pavilion in Lord's Cricket Ground, and, from its being built of wood, it burnt with such fury that the whole was reduced to a heap of ruins, before it was possible for the fire engines to render any assistance. The pavilion was, at a great expense, lately enlarged and decorated for the accommodation of the various clubs who frequent this ground; and, with the exception of the foundation, nothing now remains. There was in the pavilion a large and valuable stock of wine, the property of the subscribers, which, along with all their cricketing apparatus, now no longer exists.

MCC Presidents 1821–71. (JL)

MCC Presidents 1872–1926. (JL)

Left: MCC Presidents 1927–83. (JL)

Opposite: MCC Presidents 1984–to date. (JL)

PRESIDENTS
1984 F.G. Mann
1985 J.G.W. Davies
1986 M.C. Cowdrey
1987 J.J. Warr
1988 Field Marshal the Lord Bramall
1989 Sir Denys Roberts
1990 The Lord Griffiths
1991 M.E.L. Melluish
1992 D.R.W. Silk
1994 Sir Oliver Popplewell
1996 A.C.D. Ingleby-Mackenzie
1998 A.R. Lewis
2000 The Lord Alexander of Weedon
2001 E.R. Dexter
2002 Sir Timothy Rice
2003 C.A. Fry
2004 T.W. Graveney
2005 R.G. Marlar
2006 D.J. Insole
2007 J.M. Brearley
2008 D.L. Underwood
2009 J.R.T. Barclay
2010 C.D.A. Martin-Jenkins
2011 R.P. Hodson
2012 M.G. Griffith
2013 M.W. Gatting
2014 F.D. Morgan
2015 R.D.V. Knight
2016 M.V. Fleming
2017 The Lord MacLaurin of Knebworth
2018 A.W. Wreford
2019 K.C. Sangakkara
2021 C.J. Connor
2022 S.J. Fry
2023 M.C.J. Nicholas
1787-1820
No records remain - the fire of 28 July 1825
destroyed them.

The tenure of an MCC President is typically one year, although a few MCC Presidents have served for more than one year or have held the presidency again several years after their initial term. These include Viscount Grimston, who was President in 1837 and again in 1867 – this time as the Earl of Verulam. Grimston's last playing appearance at Lord's was for the 'Married' versus the 'Single' in June 1849. Additionally, the Marquess of Worcester served as President in 1853 and again in 1877 – this time as the Duke of Beaufort.

Lord Hawke became MCC's President in 1914 and, due to the outbreak of the First World War, held that position until he was replaced by Lord Forster in 1919. Similarly, Stanley Christopherson became President in 1939 and remained in that role until the end of the Second World War. He was succeeded by General Sir Ronald Adam in 1946. Christopherson's tenure as President of MCC is the longest on record.

HRH The Duke of Edinburgh was MCC's President in 1949 and again in 1975. Additionally, between 1992 and 1999, MCC decided to allow the presidency to last for two years instead of one. During that period, D. R. W. Silk served as President in 1992 and 1993, followed by Sir Oliver Popplewell, who held the presidency in 1994 and 1995. His replacement, A. C. D. Ingleby-Mackenzie, served in 1996 and 1997, and finally, A. R. Lewis became President in 1998, serving again in 1999.

This two-year presidency experiment was then abandoned, although Kumar Sangakkara became (in 2019) the first overseas President of MCC and, due to the impact of Covid-19, remained as President in 2020. His successor, Clare Joanne Connor, was (in 2021) the first woman to become President of MCC.

40. Bust of Frank Woolley

The MCC Committee Room also features a bust of Frank Edward Woolley, renowned as one of the finest and most elegant all-rounders in cricket history. This bust, created by Wilhelm Soukop (1907–95), a Viennese-born sculptor who died in Glasgow, dates from 1960.

Woolley was a left-handed batsman who had a first-class career lasting over thirty years, beginning in 1906, during which he scored 58,969 runs. He scored 145 centuries and took 2,066 wickets, as well as taking 1,018 catches. His averages were impressive, boasting a batting average of 40.75 and a bowling average of 19.87. Beyond these remarkable statistics, Woolley was also recognised for the way he made his runs. As a tall man, he capitalised on his long reach and impeccable timing. Furthermore, his bowling was characterised by a natural elegance.

Born on 27 May 1887 in Tonbridge, Kent, Woolley played for Kent County Cricket Club between 1906 and 1938. He first caught the attention of the Tonbridge ground staff in 1903, when he was invited to join in with the players' practice sessions. In 1904, he became a member of the ground staff and made his debut for Kent in 1906, at the age of nineteen.

In Woolley's debut season, Kent CCC secured their first County Championship title. Between 1906 and 1913, they won the championship on three other occasions. Woolley played sixty-four Test matches for England, making his debut in 1909 against South Africa. His Test career spanned approximately sixteen years, during which he scored 3,283 runs, including five centuries, with an average of thirty-six.

Soukop's bust of Frank Woolley. (JL)

In 1914, the outbreak of the First World War coincided with Woolley's peak playing ability. In that year, aged twenty-seven, he married Sybil Fordham. Their marriage lasted nearly fifty years, and they had a son and two daughters.

Following the war, Woolley resumed his career, and in 1921, during the second Test against Australia, he scored ninety-five runs and ninety-three runs in the two innings. He considered those innings among the finest of his career. Notably, Woolley was dismissed thirty-five times in the nineties throughout his career.

When he retired from cricket, Woolley became a life Member of MCC and Kent CCC and joined Kent's committee. He remained quite active into his late eighties, and in January 1971, flew to Australia to watch the last two Test matches of the series. Nine months later, in Canada, he married for a second time at the age of eighty-four, his first wife having died ten years earlier. Frank Woolley died on 18 October 1978.

WAR MEMORIALS

41. Free Foresters War Memorial

Throughout the Pavilion, several war memorial Rolls of Honour are displayed. The following five items reflect the ultimate sacrifices made by MCC Members and others associated with Lord's Ground in defence of the nation.

On the Pavilion's ground floor, at the base of the staircase leading to the Home Dressing Room, there are two Memorial Boards that honour the members of the Free Foresters who died in the two global conflicts.

The Free Foresters Cricket Club was founded by the Reverend W. K. R. Bedford in July 1856 in the Sutton Coldfield area of Warwickshire. The team adopted the name 'Free Foresters' to represent the nearby forests of Arden in Warwickshire and Needwood in Staffordshire. The 'Free' element derives from the ability of members to play against the club without permission, rather than being 'tied' to the Free Foresters. This gave rise to their motto – United though Untied.

Eighty-nine members of the Free Foresters have played for England over the years, with thirty-three of them serving as captain. Douglas Jardine, Frank Worrell, and Colin Cowdrey are among the illustrious players who have represented the club. However, since

Commemoration of the war service of the Free Foresters. (JL)

Free Foresters who died in the First and Second World Wars. (JL)

the 1970s, fewer Free Foresters have played Test cricket, although many have participated in county matches.

The boards were placed in the Pavilion due to the Free Foresters' long association with Lord's. It remains one of the leading wandering clubs in the country, boasting a membership of around 2,000 and playing approximately seventy fixtures each year.

The board on the left is headed 'The Free Foresters'. It features the Free Foresters logo, and is inscribed:

IN MEMORY
OF
THE MEMBERS OF THE FREE FORESTERS
WHO GAVE THEIR LIVES
IN
THE WORLD WARS
1914-1918 AND 1939-1945

The club's motto, 'United Though Untied', is displayed at the base of the plaque.

The plaque on the right-hand side lists the names of the Free Foresters members who lost their lives in the two world wars of the twentieth century. Among those members who perished in the First World War is one individual who was awarded the Victoria Cross.

T. Wright, VC

Theodore Wright was born on 15 May 1883 in Brighton. Educated at Clifton College and the Royal Military Academy at Woolwich, he was commissioned as a second Lieutenant on 2 October 1902.

At the age of thirty-one, Captain Theodore Wright served in the Royal Engineers during the First World War, where he was involved in combat and subsequently awarded the Victoria Cross. His citation in *The London Gazette* on 16 November 1914 reads:

> Gallantry at Mons on 23rd August in attempting to connect up the lead to demolish a bridge under heavy fire; although wounded in the head he made a second attempt. At Vailly, on 14th September, he assisted the passage of 5th Cavalry Brigade over the pontoon bridge and was mortally wounded whilst assisting wounded men into shelter.

An officer of the Scots Greys wrote in a letter:

> We got across the river the day before yesterday a bit before our time and we had to go back over a pontoon bridge considerably quicker than was pleasant, under a very heavy fire too. At the end of the bridge was an Engineer officer repairing bits blown off and putting down straw as cool as a cucumber – the finest thing I ever saw. The poor fellow was killed just after my troops got across. No man earned a better Victoria Cross.

Theodore Wright is buried at Vailly British Cemetery in France, and his medals are displayed at the Royal Engineers Museum in Gillingham, Kent.

42. First World War Roll of Honour

The period before the First World War is often regarded as cricket's 'Golden Age'. This term describes the era between the inception of the official County Championship in 1890 and the start of the First World War in 1914. It was a relatively short period dominated by a largely amateur group of players whose names still resonate today – C. B. Fry, K. S. Ranjitsinhji, and the most dominant player of the time, W. G. Grace. The Golden Age also featured several professional players, including Frank Woolley, Jack Hobbs, Wilfred Rhodes, Gilbert Jessop, and Sydney Barnes. Australians like Victor Trumper and Warwick Armstrong added to this heady mix. The writer J. B. Priestley summarised the appeal of cricket's Golden Age when he wrote in 1978, 'I cannot believe that there is another game in the world that releases so many floods of nostalgic reminiscence.'

During the First World War, Lord's Ground was requisitioned by the War Office and used for various purposes, including troop accommodation. Additionally, wireless telegraphy, cookery, and language classes were held in the Pavilion.

Following the end of hostilities in 1918, thoughts began to turn to commemorating those MCC Members who had lost their lives in the conflict. The suggestion was first raised at an MCC Committee meeting in December 1914. At the Annual General Meeting in 1915, Members were asked to assist the MCC Committee in preparing a list of those who had perished. Understandably, there was considerable post-war confusion, which delayed the completion of the list for several years. Meanwhile, the memorial's design was officially commissioned in 1920.

Initially located in the Members' Writing Room on the Pavilion's ground floor and later displayed near the entrance to the Old Library, the Roll of Honour is now positioned at the top of the South staircase of the Pavilion. MCC's First World War (1914–18) Roll of Honour is a wooden board with gold lettering that honours those Members of MCC who were killed in that conflict. Beneath it is a glazed, framed paper version of the Roll of Honour, which shows the date of a person's election to MCC membership, as well as the date and place of burial.

Originally, the Roll included two recipients of the Victoria Cross (VC), three cricketers who had played Test match cricket – K. L. Hutchings, L. J. Moon, and R. O. Schwarz – and sixty-nine others who had played first-class cricket for their counties, for MCC, or for Oxford or Cambridge.

In the early 1940s, MCC Members were further asked to compile lists for an additional Roll of Honour to commemorate those who died in the Second World War. The Roll of Honour was officially unveiled at Lord's in August 2005. By then, further research had been conducted into the First World War Roll of Honour, revealing that

First World War Roll of Honour. (JL)

thirty-eight names had been included and twenty-six excluded in error. This was not particularly surprising, given that many memorials were erected shortly after the end of the First World War. Consequently, the revised First World War board contained 330 names.

The Members of the MCC who were awarded the Victoria Cross during the First World War are listed here.

John Fitzhardinge Paul Butler, VC, DSO

Butler was an officer in the King's Royal Rifle Corps, attached to the Gold Coast Regiment of the West African Frontier Force. He died in September 1916 and is buried in Morogoro Cemetery, Tanzania. His citation, published in *The London Gazette* on 24 August 1915, read:

> For most conspicuous bravery in the Cameroons, West Africa. On 17th November, 1914, with a party of 13 men, he went into the thick bush and at once attacked the enemy, in strength about 100, including several Europeans, defeated them, and captured their machine gun and many loads of ammunition.
>
> On 27th December, 1914, when on patrol duty, with a few men, he swam the Ekam River, which was held by the enemy, alone and in the face of a brisk fire, completed his reconnaissance on the further bank, and returned in safety. Two of his men were wounded while he was actually in the water.

Captain Francis Octavius Grenfell, VC

Grenfell was a captain in the King's Royal Rifle Corps and was killed at Hooge in Belgium in May 1915. His citation appeared in *The London Gazette* on 16 November 1914 and read:

> For gallantry in action against unbroken infantry at Andregnies, Belgium, on 24th August 1914, and for gallant conduct in assisting to save the guns of the 119th Battery, Royal Field Artillery, near Doubon the same day.

Additionally, the Rt. Hon. Brigadier Sir John Smyth, Bt., VC, MC, was awarded the VC while serving with the 15th Ludhiana Sikhs on the Western Front. However, it was later discovered that Brigadier Smyth had survived the conflict. The citation for this award, published in *The London Gazette* on 29 June 1915, read:

> For most conspicuous bravery near Richebourg L'Avoue on 18th May 1915. With a bombing party of 10 men, who voluntarily undertook this duty, he conveyed a supply of 96 bombs to within 20 yards of the enemy's position over exceptionally dangerous ground, after the attempts of two other parties had failed. Lieutenant Smyth succeeded in taking the bombs to the desired position with the aid of two of his men (the other eight having been killed or wounded), and to effect his purpose he had to swim a stream, being exposed the whole time to howitzer, shrapnel, machine gun and rifle fire.

43. Second World War Roll of Honour

Directly opposite the First World War Roll of Honour is the MCC's Second World War Roll of Honour. This memorial features the names of 282 MCC Members who perished in that conflict. Commissioned in 2005, the project also included a revision of the original list from the First World War. Both boards were unveiled by Field Marshal Lord Bramall during a ceremony on 9 August 2005.

Of the 282 individuals listed on the Second World War Roll of Honour, three were recipients of the Victoria Cross, three were Test cricketers (K. Farnes, G. B. Legge, and M. J. L. Turnbull), and twenty-nine others had played first-class cricket.

The three recipients of the Victoria Cross during the Second World War are listed below.

Lieutenant-Colonel Geoffrey Charles Tasker Keyes, VC, MC, CROIX DE GUERRE

On 18 November 1941, to lift the siege of Tobruk and drive the Germans out of Cyrenaica, the British launched Operation Crusader. A small force of commandos led by Lieutenant Colonel Keyes landed from two submarines on the Libyan coast near Apollonia, situated 250 miles behind German lines. Their plan was to attack a house at Beda Littoria, located between Benghazi and Derna, which was believed to be the headquarters of the German Field Marshal Erwin Rommel. However, Rommel was not in North Africa; he was returning from a meeting in Italy. Keyes was killed in the raid, and of those who survived, all but two were captured.

Second World War Roll of Honour. (JL)

The citation in the Second Supplement to *The London Gazette* of 16 June 1942 read:

> Lieutenant-Colonel Keyes commanded a detachment of a force which landed some 250 miles behind the enemy lines to attack Headquarters, Base Installations and Communications. From the outset Lieutenant-Colonel Keyes deliberately selected for himself the command of the detachment detailed to attack what was undoubtedly the most hazardous of these objectives – the residence and Headquarters of the General Officer Commanding the German forces in North Africa. This attack, even if initially successful, meant almost certain death for those who took part in it.
>
> He led his detachment without guides, in dangerous and precipitous country and in pitch darkness, and maintained by his stolid determination and powers of leadership the morale of the detachment. He then found himself forced to modify his original plans in the light of fresh information elicited from neighbouring Arabs, and was left with only one officer and an N.C.O. with whom to break into General Rommel's residence and deal with the guards and Headquarters Staff.
>
> At zero hour on the night of 17th-18th November, 1941, having despatched the covering party to block the approaches to the house, he himself with the two others crawled forward past the guards, through the surrounding fence and so up to the house itself. Without hesitation, he boldly led his party up to the front door, beat on the door and demanded entrance. Unfortunately, when the door was opened, it was found impossible to overcome the sentry silently, and it was necessary to shoot him. The noise of the shot naturally aroused the inmates of the house and Lieutenant-Colonel Keyes, appreciating that speed was now of the utmost importance, posted the N.C.O. at the foot of the stairs to prevent interference from the floor above.
>
> Lieutenant-Colonel Keyes, who instinctively took the lead, emptied his revolver with great success into the first room and was followed by the other officer, who threw a grenade. Lieutenant-Colonel Keyes, with great daring, then entered the second room on the ground floor but was shot almost immediately on flinging open the door and fell back into the passage mortally wounded. On being carried outside by his companions, he died within a few minutes. By his fearless disregard of the great dangers which he ran and of which he was fully aware, and by his magnificent leadership and outstanding gallantry, Lieutenant-Colonel Keyes set an example of supreme self-sacrifice and devotion to duty.

Geoffrey Charles Tasker Keyes, VC, is buried in the Benghazi War Cemetery in Libya.

Captain Lord Lyell of Kinnordy, VC

Charles Antony Lyell was born on 14 June 1913 in Chelsea. As his father had died in 1918, he succeeded his grandfather as Baron Lyell in 1926. He was educated at Eton College and Christ Church, Oxford, graduating in 1936. At the age of twenty-nine, while serving as a temporary captain in the 1st Battalion, Scots Guards, the following action took place after which Lyell was recommended for the Victoria Cross.

The citation in *The London Gazette* dated 12 August 1943 provided the following details:

> From the 22nd April, 1943, to 27th April, 1943, Captain The Lord Lyell commanded his Company, which had been placed under the orders of a Battalion of the Grenadier Guards, with great gallantry, ability and cheerfulness. He led it down a slope under heavy mortar fire to repel a German counter attack on 22nd April, led it again under heavy fire through the Battalion's first objective on 23rd April in order to capture and consolidate a high point, and held this point through a very trying period of shelling, heat and shortage of water.
>
> During this period, through his energy and cheerfulness, he not only kept up the fighting spirit of his Company but also managed through Radio Telephony, which he worked himself from an exposed position, to bring most effective artillery fire to bear on enemy tanks, vehicles and infantry positions. At about 18:00 hours on 27th April, 1943, this officer's Company was taking part in the Battalion's attack on Dj Bou Arara. The Company was held up in the foothills by heavy fire from an enemy post on the left. This post consisted of an 88-millimetre gun and a heavy machine gun in separate pits. Realising that until this post was destroyed, the advance could not proceed, Lord Lyell collected the only available men not pinned down by fire – a sergeant, a lance-corporal and two guardsmen – and led them to attack it.
>
> He was a long way in advance of the others and lobbed a hand grenade into the machine gun pit, destroying the crew. At this point, his sergeant was killed, and both the guardsmen were wounded. The lance-corporal got down to give covering fire to Lord Lyell who had run straight on towards the 88-millimetre gun pit and was working his way round to the left of it. So quickly had this officer acted that he was in among the crew with the bayonet before they had time to fire more than one shot. He killed a number of them before being overwhelmed and killed himself.
>
> The few survivors of the gun crew then left the pit, some of them being killed while they were retiring, and both the heavy machine gun and 88-millimetre gun were silenced. The Company was then able to advance and take its objective. There is no doubt that Lord Lyell's outstanding leadership, gallantry and self-sacrifice enabled his Company to carry out its task, which had an important bearing on the success of the Battalion and of the Brigade.

Charles, Lord Lyell, is buried in the Massicault Commonwealth War Graves Commission (CWGC) Cemetery, located southwest of Tunis.

Captain Bernard Armitage Warburton-Lee, VC, RN

Bernard Armitage Warburton-Lee was born in September 1895 in Iscoyd, Flintshire. He attended the British Army Staff College in Camberley from 1931 to 1932.

On 10 April 1940, at the age of forty-four, Captain Bernard Warburton-Lee was aboard HMS *Hardy*, commanding the British 2nd Destroyer Flotilla during a surprise attack on German destroyers and merchant ships in Ofotfjord, Norway, in the first battle of Narvik.

Despite a blinding snowstorm, the attack was successful but was almost immediately followed by an engagement with five additional German destroyers, during which

Warburton-Lee was mortally wounded by a shell that struck HMS *Hardy*'s bridge. In June 1940, he was posthumously awarded the Victoria Cross.

The citation in the Second Supplement to *The London Gazette* dated 7 June 1940 read as follows:

> For gallantry, enterprise and daring in command of the Force engaged in the first Battle of Narvik, on the 10th of April, 1940. On being ordered to carry out an attack on Narvik, he learned from Tranoy that the enemy held the place in much greater force than had been thought. He signalled to the Admiralty that the enemy were reported to be holding Narvik in force, that six Destroyers and one Submarine were there, that the channel might be mined, and that he intended to attack at dawn, high water. The Admiralty replied that two Norwegian Coast Defence Ships might be in German hands, that he alone could judge whether to attack, and that whatever decision he made would have full support.
>
> Captain Warburton-Lee gave out the plan for his attack and led his Flotilla of five Destroyers up the Fjord in heavy snowstorms, arriving off Narvik just after daybreak. He took the enemy completely by surprise and made three successful attacks on warships and merchantmen in the harbour.
>
> The last attack was made only after anxious debate. On the Flotilla withdrawing, five enemy Destroyers of superior gun-power were encountered and engaged. The captain was mortally wounded by a shell which hit 'Hardy's' bridge. His last signal was 'Continue to engage the enemy.'

This was the first Victoria Cross to be gazetted during the Second World War. Bernard Warburton-Lee is interred in the CWGC plot at Ballangen New Cemetery, southwest of Narvik.

44. War Memorial for Non-MCC Members

Situated on the staircase near the Home Dressing Room is another war memorial. This one commemorates thirteen first-class cricketers who were not MCC Members but represented the Club in matches and lost their lives in either of the two world wars. They were all professional cricketers and were thus barred from becoming Members of MCC.

Following a campaign for recognition of these individuals, led by former England captain Michael Atherton, this Roll of Honour was unveiled jointly by Atherton and Field Marshal Lord Bramall in February 2017.

The names include four professionals who had played Test cricket – Sergeant Colin Blythe, Second Lieutenant Major William Booth, Pilot Officer G. G. Macauley, and Captain Hedley Verity*, along with four other professionals, three amateurs, and two MCC membership candidates.

The Board, topped with MCC's logo, is headed with these words:

TO THE MEMORY OF THE FIRST-CLASS CRICKETERS WHO WERE NOT MEMBERS OF M.C.C. BUT PLAYED FOR THE CLUB AND FELL DURING THE TWO WORLD WARS

Non-MCC Members killed in both world wars. (JL)

On the base of the memorial are inscribed these words:

SECURE FROM CHANGE IN THEIR HIGH-HEARTED WAYS

This sentiment, which is also displayed in the MCC's Museum, is taken from an ode written by American poet James Russell Lowell. It was first recited at the Harvard Commemoration on 21 July 1865, an event that celebrated the end of the American Civil War and honoured the Harvard alumni who had served and died in that conflict:

They come transfigured back,
Secure from change in their high-hearted ways,
Beautiful evermore, and with the rays
Of morn on their white Shields of Expectation

*Hedley Verity

Hedley Verity in bowling action. (MCC)

Hedley Verity, commemorated on this memorial, was an exceptionally effective slow left-arm bowler who represented both Yorkshire and England with great distinction.

During his career, he took 1,956 first-class wickets at an average of just 14.90. Through his contributions, Yorkshire won seven County Championships during the 1930s. His best return was a staggering 19.4–16–10–10 against Nottinghamshire in July 1932. According to eyewitness accounts, this was a world-class performance.

Verity took at least 150 wickets in each of the nine seasons in which he played. His average seasonal haul during this period was 185 wickets. His consistency and skill are unquestionable, and he can rightly be included in any list of great bowlers.

He also played in forty Test matches, taking 144 wickets at an average of 24.37 runs each. He reached 100 Test wickets faster than any other English bowler. Verity participated in four Ashes series, starting with the 1932–33 'Bodyline' series in Australia, where England won 4-1 under Douglas Jardine's captaincy. He was also part of the team in the 1934 Ashes series, during which he took fifteen wickets in the Lord's Test. Additionally, he played in the 1936–37 series and the 1938 series. Hedley Verity dismissed Don Bradman eight times in seventeen Tests, more than any other Test bowler.

During the Second World War, Captain Verity led his troops against the German army in Sicily. Verity remained at the front with his men despite suffering from dysentery. After ordering a platoon to a distant farmhouse, he instructed another to provide cover. As soon as the words were spoken, Verity was struck in the chest by a piece of shrapnel and died on 31 July 1943. The Italians honoured him with full military honours at his funeral, and his coffin was draped in the Union flag.

Fellow Yorkshireman Len Hutton led the England team to Australia for the 1954–55 Ashes series. During their journey, the boat made a stop in Italy to visit Verity's grave in the Caserta War Cemetery, where the team paid their respects.

45. Middlesex Players' War Memorial

Outside the Home Dressing Room in the Pavilion is a Memorial Board headed 'Middlesex County Cricket Club'. Just below are the words 'Roll of Honour 1914 – 1918'. The Board lists eighteen names, commemorating Middlesex cricketers who were killed in the First World War.

The lives of two individuals on the Roll of Honour are highlighted below.

Revd William Benton

When he was seventeen years old in 1890, Benton's father died, leaving him a substantial inheritance. He enlisted in the Royal Marines but deserted after a fight with a corporal. He fled to Australia under a false name, Richard White, and served in the Boer War in the Australian Artillery. After the war, Benton travelled to South Africa, where he joined the Cape Mounted Police. He then worked in a leper settlement on Robben Island, which, many years later, became Nelson Mandela's prison for over twenty-five years. Benton served there as a cook, painter, laundryman, and general handyman.

This work had a profound effect on him, and he surrendered to the authorities. After his court-martial, he served his sentence and then moved back to the United Kingdom. Following a period of study, he was ordained as a priest in 1909. However, he felt called to return to Robben Island, where he became chaplain. Later, he returned to England and became a curate at Bearsted in Kent.

In 1913, he made only two first-class appearances for Middlesex CCC. At the outbreak of the First World War, he became a military chaplain in France. He was killed in action in France on 17 August 1916, at the age of forty-three.

Reginald Oscar Schwarz, MC

Reginald Oscar Schwarz was born in South London. He was a South African Test cricketer as well as an England rugby international. Schwarz's father was born in Germany but later became a naturalised British citizen. His mother hailed from the north of England.

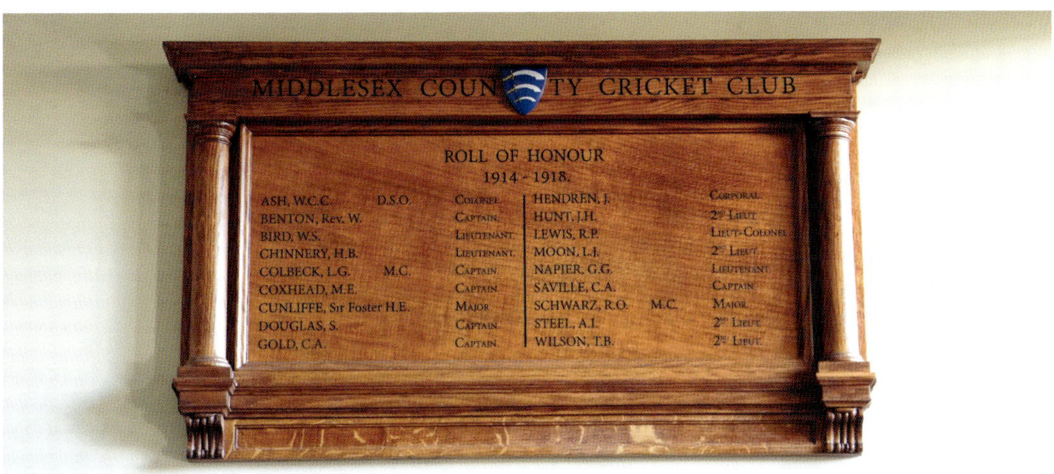

Middlesex players killed in the First World War. (JL)

Schwarz was educated at St Paul's School and Christ's College, Cambridge, but he did not complete his studies. However, he was a rugby Blue (1893) and subsequently played for Richmond while also representing Middlesex and the Barbarians. Schwarz played in three international rugby matches for England at the turn of the century, competing against Scotland in 1899 and against Ireland and Wales in 1901.

Schwarz also played cricket for Oxfordshire and Middlesex. Around 1903, he moved to South Africa to work on the Johannesburg railway. He played cricket for Transvaal and went on to play in twenty Test matches for South Africa. Schwarz became one of the key individuals responsible for the formation of the Imperial Cricket Conference (ICC). He played in four Test series against England between 1905 and 1912, taking fifty-five Test wickets at a respectable average of just over twenty-five. He was named a *Wisden* Cricketer of the Year in 1908.

At the outbreak of the First World War, he enlisted in the South African army and served in German South-West Africa. In 1916, Schwarz was in France, serving as the Deputy Assistant Quartermaster General for the 47th (London) Division of the 6th Battalion King's Royal Rifles. During this time, he was awarded the Military Cross (MC).

Schwarz suffered from poor health and was eventually transferred to the Salvage Corps. In 1918, just seven days after the Armistice, Schwarz died of pneumonia after contracting the Spanish flu. He is buried in Étaples Military Cemetery.

CRICKET HONOURS BOARDS

46. Home Dressing Room – One Day International Honours Board

The Home Dressing Room at Lord's is situated on the first floor of the Pavilion's southern end. Within the dressing room, three Honours Boards commemorate outstanding performances at Lord's.

First, immediately above the arch leading to the players' balcony, is an Honours Board that records the players who have excelled in One Day Internationals (ODIs). On the left-hand side, the players who have scored 100 runs or more in an ODI at Lord's are listed, beginning with Dennis Amiss's 137 runs in 1975 against India. That innings came four years after the first-ever ODI in Australia in January 1971*.

*1971 – First One Day International

The first-ever ODI was played during the 1970–71 MCC tour to Australia. The first three days of the third Test at Melbourne had been washed out due to rain. Officials decided that the Test match should be abandoned and that a one-off One Day International match would be played between Australia and MCC (England) at the Melbourne Cricket Ground.

The match took place in front of 46,000 spectators on 5 January 1971. It consisted of forty overs per innings, with each over comprising eight balls. The teams wore their usual white clothing, and a red ball was used. Australia won the game by five wickets. John Edrich (MCC) was the top scorer, having scored eighty-two runs off 119 deliveries.

Just two players have multiple appearances on the ODI Honours Board in the Home Dressing Room. Marcus Trescothick has three centuries – in 2001, 2002, and 2003 – and Graham Gooch scored hundreds in both 1985 and 1989. The highest score was recorded by England's Claire Taylor, who scored 156 runs (not out) in a women's ODI against India in 2006.

To the right of the doors are players who have taken five or more wickets in a single ODI. The performances recorded in cream-coloured rectangles relate to women's ODIs, with the most notable being Anya Shrubsole's 6-46 in the 2017 women's World Cup Final against India.

The ODI Honours Board in the Home Dressing Room. (JL)

47. Home Dressing Room – Test Match Honours Board

The second, and certainly the best-known, is the Test match Honours Board. This board commemorates the performances of English players who have scored a Test century at Lord's or have taken at least five wickets in a Test innings, or ten in a match. Currently, all the names on this Board are those of male cricketers, as a women's Test match has never been played at Lord's. However, one is scheduled for 2026 between England and India.

Players on Both Boards (Batting and Bowling) in the Home Dressing Room

In total, eight players have their names listed in both the batting and bowling sections of the Test match Honours Board in the Home Dressing Room.

George 'Gubby' Allen was the first to double up when, in 1931, he scored 122 in a drawn match against New Zealand. His appearance on the bowling Honours Board came in 1936 when he took five wickets in each innings of a Test match against India.

Raymond Illingworth of Yorkshire was next when, in 1967, he took 6-29 against India. Two years later, in 1969, Illingworth scored 113 in a drawn match against the West Indies. Two other Yorkshiremen – Geoff Boycott and John Hampshire – also made centuries in that match.

There was a nine-year gap before the next player got his name on both sides of the Board. The Somerset all-rounder Ian Botham achieved this feat in the same match against Pakistan in 1978, scoring 108 runs and taking 8-34. Botham subsequently appeared on the bowling Honours Board six more times – once more in 1978, as well as in 1979, 1982, twice in 1984, and finally in 1985.

Test batting – Home Dressing Room. (JL)

Test bowling – Home Dressing Room. (JL)

Another lengthy gap followed until Andrew Flintoff achieved the feat in 2003 and 2009. He scored 142 in the 2003 Test match against South Africa and completed the double with a match-winning 5-92 against Australia in 2009.

In his early days in the England team, Stuart Broad was regarded as an all-rounder, confirmed when he scored 169 against Pakistan in 2010. His bowling successes came later with five-wicket hauls against the West Indies in 2012, New Zealand in 2013, and Ireland in 2023.

Ben Stokes's first hundred in a Lord's Test match came in the 2015 fixture against New Zealand. Further hundreds followed for Stokes in the 2019 Ashes Test against Australia and the 2023 fixture against the same team. In 2017, Stokes made his only appearance to date on the bowling Honours Board with figures of 6-22 against the West Indies.

In 2016, Chris Woakes was recorded on the bowling Honours Board with match figures of 11-102 against Pakistan. He followed this up in 2018 with a century against India and made another appearance on the bowling Board in 2019 during the Test match against Ireland.

In the 2024 season, Gus Atkinson became the eighth person to join this illustrious group. In his first season as a Test player, he took twelve wickets in the match against the West Indies and five wickets in the Test against Sri Lanka. Additionally, he scored a century against Sri Lanka.

Most Appearances on the Batting Honours Board

Eight times Joe Root – 2013, 2014, 2017, 2021, 2022, 2024 (twice), and 2025

Seven times Graham Gooch – 1980, 1986 (twice), 1987*, 1990 (twice), and 1991 – **the 1987 appearance was during the Bicentenary Test for MCC against the Rest of the World. Although it was not an official Test match, it is included here.*

I spoke to Graham Gooch about what it meant to a cricketer to appear on the Honours Boards at Lord's. He told me, 'Players obviously want to do exceptionally well at the Home of Cricket. But what they really want is to have their name up there with all the greats of the game, their name marked down for eternity in history at the finest cricket ground in the world.'

Six times Michael Vaughan
Five times Andrew Strauss and Kevin Pietersen
Four times Ian Bell, Allan Lamb, and Alastair Cook

Nine players have made three appearances on the batting Honours Board, and fifteen have made two.

Most Appearances on the Bowling Honours Board

Seven times Ian Botham and James Anderson
Five times Fred Trueman
Four times Derek Underwood
Three times Brian Statham, Bob Willis, Stuart Broad, and Chris Woakes

Angus Fraser is one of eight players with two appearances on the bowling Honours Board. He told me, 'It means a lot to be on the Board – there are some great bowlers on there, and that in the visitors' dressing room. It's a case of your name being there in 50+ years and people still remembering you and talking about you. There is something at Lord's that recognises you put in a couple of very good performances on one of cricket's greatest stages.'

Thirteen players have taken five wickets in each innings of a Test match; however, their achievements are recorded with a single entry. This group includes Hedley Verity, Derek Underwood, and Ian Botham.

The match that generated the most appearances on the Boards occurred in July 1990, when England played India*.

*1990 – England v India

In England's first innings, there were three centurions – Graham Gooch with 333, Allan Lamb with 139, and Robin Smith, who scored 100 not out. India's first innings concluded with two more centurions – Ravi Shastri with 100 and Mohammed Azharuddin with 121. Angus Fraser took 5-104 in that innings. During England's second innings, Graham Gooch scored a second century – 123. This high-scoring Test match was won by England by 274 runs.

- 1,603 runs were scored in the match, which at that time was the highest aggregate score at Lord's in a Test match. This surpassed the previous record from 1930, when 1,601 runs were made. K. S. Duleepsinhji scored 173, and Don Bradman scored 254 in that match.
- Graham Gooch's 333 in the first innings remains the highest individual Test match score at Lord's since Walter Hammond's 240 in 1938.
- Graham Gooch scored a total of 456 runs in the match, making it the highest individual aggregate in Test cricket at Lord's. Only two other players have scored over 400 in a Test match: Mark Taylor (334 not out and 92) at Peshawar in 1998, and Brian Lara, who achieved the only quadruple century in Test cricket against England at St John's in 2004.
- Twenty-four runs in one over by Kapil Dev off Eddie Hemmings to avoid the follow-on – the most runs ever scored in a single over in a Test match at Lord's.
- Seven players were added to the Honours Boards: Gooch (twice), Lamb, Smith, Fraser, Shastri, and Azharuddin; the most additions in a single match at Lord's.
- 653 was England's highest score against India, surpassing the total from the match in Madras five years earlier. It was also England's highest total at Lord's.

Four matches at Lord's have resulted in six additions to the Honours Boards, while a further seventeen matches have contributed five more.

48. Home Dressing Room – Middlesex Captains

Finally, surrounding the window is a list of Middlesex CCC captains. Middlesex County Cricket Club has been a tenant at Lord's Ground since the 1860s. Notable Middlesex

Middlesex captains since 1864. (JL)

captains include many former England captains, such as Mike Gatting, Andrew Strauss, George 'Gubby' Allen, and Mike Brearley. In recent years, captains from all formats have also been included.

49. Visitors' Dressing Room – One Day International Honours Board

At the far end of the corridor leading from the Home Dressing Room is the Dressing Room used by visiting teams. Many overseas cricketers aspire to play at Lord's Ground, knowing they will enter this Dressing Room and then take that famous walk down the stairs, through the Long Room, past the MCC Members, and out onto the hallowed turf.

The ODI Honours Board is positioned above the arch leading to the players' balcony. Once again, there are two sections: on the left, the names of players who have scored at least 100 runs in a single ODI innings at Lord's are displayed, and on the right, the names of players who have taken at least five wickets in an ODI innings at Lord's are shown. The cream-coloured rectangles signify women cricketers.

Clive Lloyd, the West Indian captain, was the first player to appear on the batting side of the ODI Board, scoring a century in the 1975 World Cup Final against Australia.

Only two women's names are recorded on the Visitors' ODI Honours Board – Lisa Keightley and Cathryn Fitzpatrick, both Australians, for their performances in the same match against England in 1998.

Another World Cup match in 2019 produced the highest number of appearances on the ODI Honours Board in a single match. Pakistan played Bangladesh, and the performances

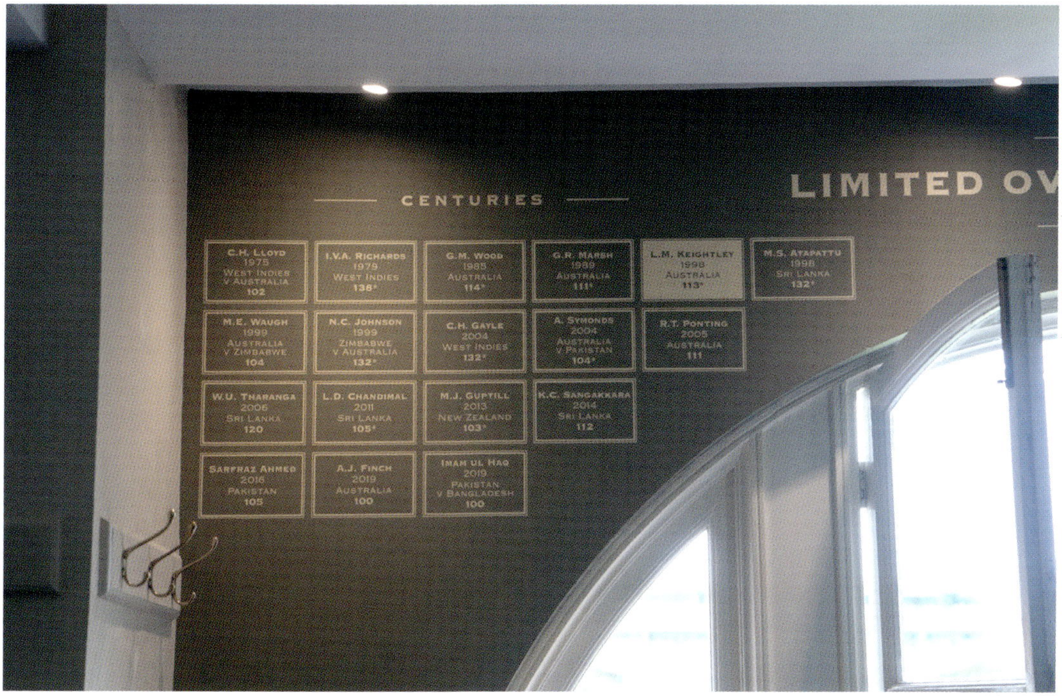

ODI batting – Visitors' Dressing Room. (JL)

ODI bowling – Visitors' Dressing Room. (JL)

of three players – Imam-ul-Haq of Pakistan, Mustafizur Rahman of Bangladesh, and Shaheen Afridi of Pakistan – are recorded.

Brett Lee of Australia is the only player with two appearances on the ODI Honours Board in the Visitors' Dressing Room. He achieved this by taking at least five wickets in matches in 2005 and 2009.

50. Visitors' Dressing Room – Test Match Honours Board

The Test match Honours Board in the Visitors' Dressing Room is divided into two sections. On the left, closest to the windows, four panels commemorate visiting players who have scored at least 100 runs in a Test match innings at Lord's. To the right, nearest to the dressing room door, three panels display the names of visiting bowlers who have taken at least five wickets in a Test match innings or ten wickets in a single Test match.

In 1998, a tradition began in the Visitors' Dressing Room at Lord's. During the England vs. South Africa Test match, renowned fielder Jonty Rhodes scored a century. Although he was known for his excellence in fielding, he also wanted to be recognised as a batsman. When he returned to the Dressing Room after his innings, he took a length of tape, wrote the following, and attached it to the Honours Board:

1998 J. N. RHODES 117
(BATSMAN/NOT FIELDER)

Following Jonty Rhodes's example, Allan Donald did the same by adding:

1998 A. A. DONALD 5-32
(NOW FOR 10)

Attached to the pieces of tape is a black armband. Jonty Rhodes told me that the South African players wore these to honour a former South African captain, Jackie McGlew, who had died on 8 June 1998.

These pieces of tape, along with all subsequent pieces, remain on the Honours Boards until the official signwriters arrive, typically a day or so after the match concludes. MCC's Museum has around seventy additional examples.

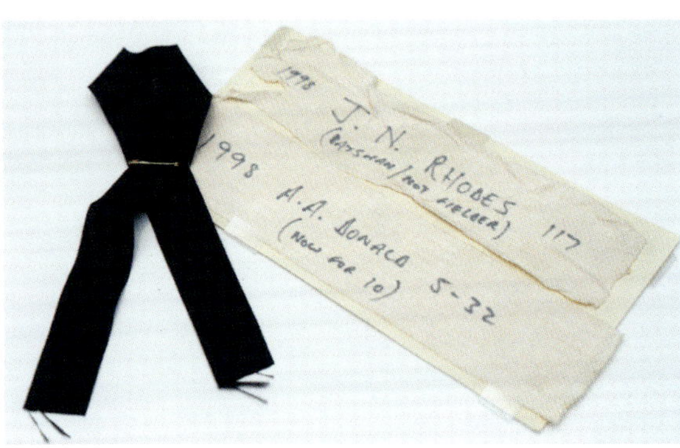

Honours Board tape – Jonty Rhodes and Allan Donald. (JL)

Test batting – Visitors' Dressing Room. (JL)

Test bowling – Visitors' Dressing Room. (JL)

All the cricket Honours Boards at Lord's date from around 1990, with information added retrospectively, going back to 1884. The current Boards are larger and were commissioned in 2018 to replace the original, smaller versions, which were filling up rapidly. The original Boards were removed and destroyed. It was felt that, since the Honours Boards are for the players, having another version still in existence would dilute the impact.

In the early years of Test match cricket – between 1889 and 1930 – the only Test-playing visitors to Lord's who appeared on the Honours Board in the Visitors' Dressing Room were players representing Australia and South Africa. Since 1930, players from other countries started to feature.

Twelve countries currently hold Test status. The first official Test match was contested between Australia and England in March 1877. These two Test-playing nations were joined by South Africa in 1889. Next to enter the group were the West Indies in 1928, New Zealand in 1930, and India in 1932. A further six nations joined the Test-playing club after the Second World War: Pakistan in 1952, Sri Lanka in 1982, Zimbabwe in 1992, Bangladesh in 2000, Ireland in 2018, and Afghanistan, also in 2018, completing the set. Except for Afghanistan, all the Test-playing countries have representatives on the Honours Boards.

Players Not on Either Board in the Visitors' Dressing Room

Many legendary cricketers, including Bradman, Gavaskar, Hadlee, and Miller, have their names inscribed on the Honours Boards at Lord's. Surprisingly, great players such as Jacques Kallis, Brian Lara, Ricky Ponting, Virat Kohli, and Sachin Tendulkar have not scored a century at Lord's in a Test match against England. Additionally, famous bowlers including Shane Warne, Dennis Lillee, Jeff Thomson, Anil Kumble, Wasim Akram, Imran Khan, Curtly Ambrose, and Muttiah Muralitharan have never taken five wickets in a Test match innings at the Ground. Only male players' names appear on the Boards, as there has never been a women's Test match at Lord's.

Players on Both Visitors' Honours Boards

Only three players appear on both sides of the Honours Board in the Visitors' Dressing Room for batting and bowling. The first to achieve this feat was Mulvantrai Himmatlal 'Vinoo' Mankad in the 1952 Test match against England, where he scored 184 and took 5-196.

The next was the great Australian cricketer Keith Miller, who scored a century in the 1953 Ashes Test at Lord's. This was followed by his performance in the 1956 Test match when he took five wickets in each innings against England. Keith Miller also scored two centuries in the 'Victory Tests' in 1945, following the Second World War, but they are not recognised as official Test matches.

The most recent player to gain recognition on both boards was Garfield Sobers. He scored his first century at Lord's for the West Indies during the 1966 Test match and added a second in 1973. Furthermore, in 1970, Sobers scored 183 and took 6-21 for the Rest of the World against England*.

*1970 – England v Rest of the World XI

South Africa was scheduled to tour England in 1970 after defeating Australia 4-0 in a series held in South Africa. However, following the D'Oliveira affair in 1968, opposition to the tour intensified due to increasing resistance against the South African government's apartheid policy. A determined group, including John Arlott and Mike Brearley, launched a campaign to prevent the tour.

The UK Government asked the Test and County Cricket Board (TCCB) to cancel the tour. They reluctantly agreed, and the invitation to the South African team was withdrawn, resulting in the possibility of no international cricket in England in 1970 and an inevitable loss of revenue.

As a result of these events, a 'Rest of the World' team was quickly assembled for a five-match series starting at Lord's. Captained by Garfield Sobers, the World XI won that Test comfortably – by an innings and eighty runs – and the series by 4–1. Garfield Sobers was the standout performer in the first match at Lord's with figures of 6-21 on the first morning and a century later in the game.

At the time, this five-match series was officially recognised as a Test series by *Wisden*. However, the International Cricket Conference (ICC) changed its status in 1972, concluding that the matches should be regarded as 'first-class' rather than Test matches. Consequently, Alan Jones of Glamorgan, who was awarded his Test cap for his debut in this match, had it withdrawn later. On the fiftieth anniversary of that match, the ECB decided to present Jones with a new England Test cap – number 696 – the next available after Zak Crawley had been awarded number 695 the previous November. The presentation was made in a virtual ceremony attended by, among others, ECB chair Colin Graves, England Test captain Joe Root, former England captain and Glamorgan teammate Tony Lewis, and Glamorgan CEO Hugh Morris.

Neutral Test Matches

Aside from a triangular international tournament between England, Australia, and South Africa that took place in 1912, the next neutral Test match at Lord's occurred in 2010, when Australia faced Pakistan. Australians Shane Watson and Marcus North are recognised on the bowling Honours Board for their contributions in this match, part of a series comprising two Tests and two T20 matches that the Pakistan cricket team played against Australia in England during July 2010. Although Pakistan was the official 'home' side, the tour was staged in England due to security issues in Pakistan.

In June 2025, South Africa played Australia in the final of the ICC World Test Championship at Lord's. The match saw three new entries on the Test match Honours Boards. In the Home Dressing Room, performances by South African players Aiden Markram (scoring 136) and Kagiso Rabada (achieving 5-51) were recorded, while Australian captain Pat Cummins (with 6-28) is honoured in the Visitors' Dressing Room.

Most Appearances on Visitors' Honours Boards

If an overseas player is fortunate during their career as a Test cricketer, they might play three Test matches at Lord's against England. Sachin Tendulkar was unusual in that he played five Tests at Lord's without appearing once on the Honours Board. In contrast, Dilip Vengsarkar played three Test matches for India at Lord's and scored three centuries: the first in 1979, the second in 1982, and his final century in 1986. A number of visiting players have scored two centuries in Test match cricket at Lord's, including Don Bradman, Garfield Sobers, Gordon Greenidge, and Steve Smith.

There is some debate regarding the presentation of bowling figures on the Honours Boards in both Dressing Rooms. While batsmen's centuries are recorded individually, bowlers' totals are combined. For instance, George Headley scored a century in each innings in the 1939 Test match and received two entries on the Board. Conversely, Bob Massie, who took eight wickets in each innings for Australia in 1972, received only one entry.

On the bowling Honours Board, the most successful visiting Test match bowlers are Richard Hadlee of New Zealand and Australia's Glenn McGrath, each with three appearances on the Board. Hadlee is recorded in 1976, 1983, and 1986, while McGrath is listed in 1997, 2000, and 2004. Those with two appearances on the bowling Board include Ray Lindwall, Malcolm Marshall, and Allan Donald.

The following players took five wickets in each innings of a Test match, with their achievements recorded in a single entry:

Charles Turner (Australia)	1888
Sonny Ramadhin (West Indies)	1950
Keith Miller (Australia)	1956
Bob Massie (Australia)	1972
Andy Roberts (West Indies)	1976
Dion Nash (New Zealand)	1994
Makhaya Ntini (South Africa)	2002

1987 – MCC v Rest of the World XI

The MCC Bicentenary match took place at Lord's Ground in late August 1987. Designated as a five-day, first-class cricket exhibition match, it was staged to commemorate the MCC's 200th anniversary. Mike Gatting captained MCC's team, while Allan Border led the Rest of the World side.

Graham Gooch, Mike Gatting, and West Indian batsman Gordon Greenidge scored centuries for MCC. As a result, Greenidge became the first player whose name appears on the Test match Honours Boards in both the Home and Visitors' Dressing Rooms. Kagiso Rabada became the second in June 2025 in the final of the ICC World Test Championship.

Sunil Gavaskar, in his final match, scored a century for the Rest of the World. Although the match did not have Test status, these individual performances were recorded on the Lord's Honours Boards. Due to rain on the final day, the match ended in a draw.

EXTRAS

In this final section, I am (rather shamelessly) using the cricketing term 'Extras' to add a few more to the fifty. For example, Lord's Ground is home to around 100 memorial benches that commemorate the lives of MCC and Middlesex Members. They can be seen dotted around the Ground and adjacent to the Coronation Garden. Some famous cricketers have been honoured in this way by their families and friends, including Patsy Hendren, Bill Edrich, and Fred Titmus.

At Lord's, I work with colleagues to guide visitors through significant areas of the Ground, including the Media Centre, the Players' Dressing Rooms, and the Long Room – the most famous room in cricket and possibly the most famous room in all sport. The

Benches around the Coronation Garden. (JL)

The Long Room in the Lord's Pavilion. (JL)

Long Room is home to several of MCC's most important paintings and serves as the players' entry point to the field of play. I cannot conclude without sharing a photograph of this remarkable space.

For well over 200 years, much of cricket's history has been written and commemorated at Lord's Ground in St John's Wood. From the cricketing exploits of W. G. Grace, Denis Compton, Ian Botham, and Ben Stokes to some of cricket's more controversial episodes – the fallout following the 'Bodyline' series in the early 1930s, discussions surrounding the D'Oliveira affair in the late 1960s, and the whole debate surrounding Kerry Packer's World Series Cricket in the mid-1970s.

More stories will undoubtedly be written about Thomas Lord's historic old Ground. Additionally, a few mysteries remain to be solved, such as the identities of the eight individuals portrayed in stone on the front of the Pavilion. The heads are depicted in a caricature style, looking out onto the outfield from the middle balcony. It is believed that Spencer Ponsonby-Fane and Lord Harris are among them, while the others may represent the MCC Committee members at the time of the Pavilion's construction. The original designs were lost in a fire some time ago, so we may never know for sure.

Finally, considering the influence and importance of Lord's Ground in the history of the game, I would like to conclude with the words of Harry Surtees Altham, MCC's President in 1959. Speaking at MCC's 150th anniversary in 1964 about being at the present Ground, he reflected on Thomas Lord and his legacy:

> How little can his father, when he rode north from Yorkshire to stake his life and fortune for Prince Charlie at Culloden, how little can his son, as he bowled away in the open fields at Islington at the members of the White Conduit Club – how little can either of them have imagined what the family name and the ground that bears it would come to mean to all the world today: a focus of tradition and history for a game that, like Ariel, has fetched a girdle round the earth, a cement of loyalties and of friendships, and a symbol of values constant and unchallengeable in a changing and challenging world.

BIBLIOGRAPHY

Arlott, John, *Arlott on Cricket*, (London: Willow Books, 1984)

Cardus, Neville, *Autobiography* (William Collins Sons & Co., 1949)

Compton, Denis, *Playing for England* (London: Sampson Low, Marston & Co. Ltd, 1948)

Frith, David, *Bodyline Autopsy* (London: Aurum Press Ltd, 2003)

Doggart, Hubert, *The Heart of Cricket* (London: Hutchinson & Co., 1967)

Green, Benny, *The Lord's Companion* (London: Pavilion Books Ltd, 1987)

Green, Stephen, *Lord's The Cathedral of Cricket* (Stroud: Tempus Publishing, 2003)

Harris, Lord and Ashley-Cooper, F. S., *Lord's and the M.C.C.* (London: Herbert Jenkins Ltd, 1923)

Hart-Davis, Duff, *Pavilions of Splendour* (London: Methuen Publishing Ltd, 2004)

Knight, Albert E., *The Complete Cricketer* (London: Methuen and Co., 1906)

Lewis, Tony, *A Summer of Cricket* (London: Pelham Books, 1976)

Marshall, John, *Lord's* (London, Pelham Books Ltd, 1969)

Pracy, David, *Gentlemen and Players of Essex* (draft)

Rait-Kerr, Diana and Peebles, Ian, *Lord's 1946-1970* (London: George G. Harrop and Co. Ltd, 1971)

Rice, Tim, *Treasures of Lord's* (London: William Collins Sons & Co. Ltd, 1989)

Robertson-Glasgow, R. C., *46 Not Out* (London: Broadwater Press, 1948)

Swanton, E. W., *Cricket from all Angles* (Michael Joseph Ltd, 1968)

Times, The, *M.C.C. 1787-1937* (London: The Times Publishing Co. Ltd, 1937)

Warner, P. F., *The Book of Cricket* (London: J. M. Dent & Sons Ltd, 1911)

Warner, Sir Pelham, *Lord's 1787-1945* (London: George G. Harrop and Co. Ltd, 1946)

Williams, Marcus (Ed.), *Double Century, 200 Years of Cricket in The Times* (William Collins and Sons, 1985)

Additionally, the following websites have been referenced:

www.abc.net.au
www.britishnewspaperarchive.co.uk
www.canalmuseum.org.uk
www.cricbuzz.com
www.cricketweb.net
www.cricmash.com
www.espncricinfo.com
www.freeforesters.com
www.gloscricket.co.uk
www.historic-uk.com

www.howstat.com
www.lords.org
www.oldframlinghamian.com
www.paulfrasercollectibles.com
www.portmanestate.co.uk
www.prabook.com
www.reptonchurch.uk
www.roberthuntsculpture.com
www.scotsguards.org
www.sportsadda.com
www.thegazette.co.uk
www.vcgca.org
www.visitstainedglass.uk
www.wikipedia.org
www.wisden.com

ACKNOWLEDGEMENTS

Thanks to Jed Leicester for his exceptional photography. Jed's photos are marked with (JL) in the captions. Additionally, gratitude is extended to Neil Robinson (Head of Heritage and Collections, Marylebone Cricket Club) and his team for the other photographs (indicated as MCC) and for their invaluable fact-checking. Further thanks are due to Neil, and to Roland Butcher (Middlesex CCC and England), who kindly provided the Forewords.

Appreciation also goes to Robert Hunt (Honorary Secretary and Trustee, The Society of Portrait Sculptors), Antony Dufort (Fellow of the Royal Society of Sculptors) who also provided a photograph of his sculpture, Graham Gooch (Essex CCC and England), Angus Fraser (Middlesex CCC and England), and Jonty Rhodes (South Africa), who all shared insights into their roles in the history of Lord's Cricket Ground.

This project would not have been possible without the support of Nick Grant, Jenny Bennett, and the team at Amberley Publishing, whose guidance in constructing this book I sincerely appreciate. I also extend my gratitude to the generations of cricket writers and thinkers who have unknowingly contributed to this work. The Bibliography at the end of the book is a modest nod to their contributions.

Finally, I would like to thank my son, Ian, and especially my wife, Anna, for their unwavering support throughout this endeavour. They offered ideas, constructive feedback, and proofreading help throughout the process. Thank you!